AF541769

WOMEN EMPOWERMENT

WOMEN EMPOWERMENT

Edited by

Dr. Rajib Lochan Panigrahy
Lecturer
(Computer Science)
Swami Sivananda Polytechnic
Aska–761 110 (Orissa)

&

Dr. Dasarathi Bhuyan
Head
Dept. of Political Science
Belaguntha Science College
Belaguntha
Ganjam (Orissa)

DISCOVERY PUBLISHING HOUSE
NEW DELHI-110002

First Published-2006

Reprinted: 2013

ISBN 81-8356-087-3

Published by

DISCOVERY PUBLISHING HOUSE

4831/24, Ansari Road, Prahlad Street,
Darya Ganj, New Delhi-110002 (India)
Phone: 23279245 • Fax: 91-11-23253475
E-mail:dphtemp@indiatimes.com

Printed at: Dynamic printers, Delhi

Preface

Women constitute nearly half of total population of the country. Therefore, the development of the country is not possible without the development of this vast segment. For centuries women in India are suffering due to discrimination, exploitation and exposed to various kinds of harassment at various levels. Empowerment of women implies process by which women's power of self-organisation is promoted and reinforced, they develop the capacity for self-reliance out crossing the relationship of subordinates on account of gender, social and economic status and society.

UN observed the year 1975 as the International Year for Women. International Women's Day comes and passes off quietly every year. Much fanfare is created in seminars, workshops, newspapers where pundits vehemently present articles/papers and address the flamboyant issue of women empowerment. This has been happening ever seen the coining of the term 'women empowerment'. Yet women has not achieved total emancipation.

Women should be conscious about their rights, privileges, status, position, etc. She is the mother of the race and liaison with the generations. She is not only the symbol and source of progress, but she can mould the future of the nation also. Women are making efforts round the world to see that their rights and respected, voices heeded, their opportunities widened. The voice from the kitchen is being heard in international forum. They should be bought into the mainstream of national development not as beneficiaries but as contributors and partakers along with men, and as write to claimant of social security. Let us all strive to give women the place they show richly and rightfully deserve in society. There are no one person or institution or agency, which alone empowers women. The creation of an enabling environment through strong polity support, the work of voluntary organisations/NGOs, women's groups, committed bureaucrats and other support groups are among the multitude of agents who can provide support to take forward the agenda of women empowerment. Besides these above agents, the thought provoking writings of academicians and researchers are the most formidable agents or forces, which facilitate the process of women empowerment.

The purpose of this book is to invigorate and actuate the notion of women empowerment. This book contains 13 articles/papers by senior political scientists, economists as well as young upcoming lecturers, research scholars, advocates from different parts of the country. This is a unique cooperative venture where the contributors of articles/papers have joined hand in giving a sturdy support in the process of women empowerment. We take this opportunity to think all the contributors of articles/papers published in this book; Shri Tilak Wasan, Proprietor of Discovery Publishing House, New Delhi for publishing this book. Without this assistance, it may not see the daylight.

—Editors

List of Contributors

1. **Dr. Bandana Gaur** is a Senior Lecturer of Faculty of Social Sciences, Department of Sociology, DEI, Dayalbagh, Agra, UP.

2. **Dr. Nilanchala Muni** is a Reader of Political Science in K.S.U.B. College, Bhanjanagar under Behrampur University having IGNOU study center for various courses.

3. **Dr. Bishnu Narayan Sethi** is a Lecturer in Economics in L.N. Degree College, Kodala under Berhampur University.

4. **Mr. Santosh Kumar Pradhan** M.A. (Economics), LL.B. is a lawyer at Aska, former Block Coordinator of Hindustan Latex Family Planning Promotion Trust (HLFPPT) sponsored by Ministry of Health and Family Welfare, Government of India at Aska Block. He is a Research Scholar of Berhampur University on Child Labour in Agriculture Sector.

5. **Smt. Anjali Das** is a Senior Faculty of Management Studies, Department of Economics, College of Business Administration, Behrampur under Berhampur University, Orissa.

6. **Subhrabala Behera** (M.A, M.Phil., CT) is a Lecturer in Political Science, KPAN College, Bankoi, Khurdha Dist. Orissa under Utkal University.

7. **Mr. Laxmi Narayan Panda** (B.Sc., M.Ed.) Science Teacher of Girls' High School, Balimela, Malkanagiri.

8. **Mr. Uma Sankar Das** has qualified in M.A (Economics), LL.B., PGDRD. He is working as District Project Coordinator for the District of Ganjam, Khurdha, Phulabni and Nayagarh in Health Village Project (sponsored by Govt. of India), HLFPPT.

9. **Dr. B. Eswar Rao Pattnayak** is a Reader in Economics of Sashi Bhusan Rath Government Womens' College, Berhampur under Berhampur University of Orissa.

10. **Govinda Chandra Panda** is working as Lecturer & Head, Department of Economics, A.M.C.S. College, Tikabali, Kandhamal, Orissa. He is the author of a dozon of articles, attended and participated in many state level and national seminars in India.He is doing Ph.D. on Tribal Women.

11. **Deepak Bishoyi** (M.A. in Economics, M.Phil.) is a Research Scholar of Berhampur University on the topic of Tourism in Orissa.

Contents

1

Empowerment of Women in Orissa

A Case Study of Koraput District

Dr. B. Eswar Rao Patnaik

SECTION–I

Introducion

Women constitute a unique resource of a nation. It needs recognition that, women are the builders and molders of a nation's destiny. In rural areas, women perform a major part of agricultural operations like, breaking clods of earth, manuring, weeding, transplanting, harvesting and threshing. They are busy in domestication (care) of diary animals and small industries like pottery, rope and basket making, food processing and handloom weaving. So, it follows that, the burden shared by the women for the socio-economic development in two fold, one on the domestic front and the other on the economic front. According to an ILO estimation, women who constitute half of the world's population, perform two-thirds of the world's work, receive on tenth of its income and own less than one hundredth of its property. It is evident, therefore that in practice, we depart from the principle of gender equality, though economic development can be seen in terms of expansion of opportunities and choices that the Individuals in the society enjoy (Jean Droze and Amartyasen, 1997).

The declaration of international women's decade in 1975 has brought to forefront the role of women as major partners in development of an economy. The pendulum of India economy began oscillating from "welfare" to "development" of women in the Sixth Five Year (1980-85). The Ninth Plan (1997-2002) has opened the doors for the welcome guest of empowerment of women, through convergence of existing services available in both women-specific and women-related sectors. The word empowerment has been defined by the World Bank as the process of increasing the capacity of individuals or groups to make choices and transform those choices into desired actions and outcomes. Central to this process are actions which both build individual and collective assets and improve the efficiency and fairness of the organizational and institutional context which govern the use of these assets. At individual level, empowerment of women centers round three variables, namely health, education and empowerment.

A Case Study

The present chapter is a study of undivided Koraput District, one of the backward districts of Orissa. The author wants to acquaint the reader with the contribution of women to the development of a rural economy in a hilly and inaccessible region. The analysis may be important both for analytical and policy related reasons. The study is based on primary and secondary data.

The multi-stage random sampling technique was followed in field investigation. Five percentage of villages in three blocks i.e. Narayanpur, Kotpad, Jeypore block (17 blocks) were selected for enquiry. For each sampled village a list of all households were prepared and 20% households from each village were selected through systematic random sampling procedure giving a total of 389 households. The data collected related to 1987-88 agricultural year. The figures obtained from field studies were tabulated through arithmetic average and they were compared with corresponding average of the district in 2001.

The academic exercise concentrates on three areas, education, employment (work participation rate) and agriculture for empowering women.

Characteristics of the Region

As per the sample survey 1987, out of 389 households, 66 families (16.96%) comprised General Category population, 229 households (58.87%) households have ST background, 94 families (24.16%) hail from SC population. The percentage share of SC and ST populations in the undivided Koraput district was 69.31% of the total population. The corresponding average at state level was 38.41%. Prof. N.B. Pradhan (2005) has argued that, the incidence of poverty in 1999-2000 among ST population in Orissa is the highest 73.08%.

Out of a total population of 2331, covered by the study, male population comprised 1242 and the number of females was 1089 in 17 sample villages. The finding seems to confirm the fact that, the sex ratio is adverse in Koraput region as well as Orissa province. There has been an improvement in the total population of the district from 1029577 in 1991 to 1177954 in 2001. The sex ratio, is not titled in favour of female population and it has come down from 998 in 1991 to 972 in 2001, the incidence of high infant mortality rate explain the observed trend.

Women empowerment is complicated by the fact that in Orissa there is a strong preference for male child compared to girl child, as sons are considered as bread winners of the family. Gender bias continues in respect of sharing of food by family members and medical treatment for boys and girls during periods of indifferent health. E.R. Patnaik and B.C. Mohapatro (1980) have reasoned that, access to education in low income families are mostly sex-specific. It is frequently the male child who continues with his education, while the female child drops out top substitute work for schooling. Arndhati Chattopadhya (2005) has identified grinding poverty as an impediment in the path of empowerment of women. While the current scholar has enumerated that the average per capita income of a person was Rs. 112 per month in Koraput district in 1987, the Orissa Development Report 2004 by Planning Commission issued by Government of India has succinctly observed that, a vast segment of population of KBK district did not have a per capita monthly income of Rs. 500.

Poor health status of women fold is accounted for by abysmal poverty, want of balanced diet in their consumption pattern, limited access to medical services, gender discrimination and splendor work participation rate among females.

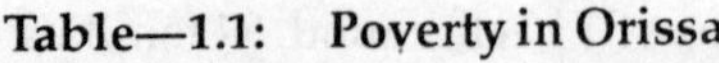

Table—1.1: Poverty in Orissa

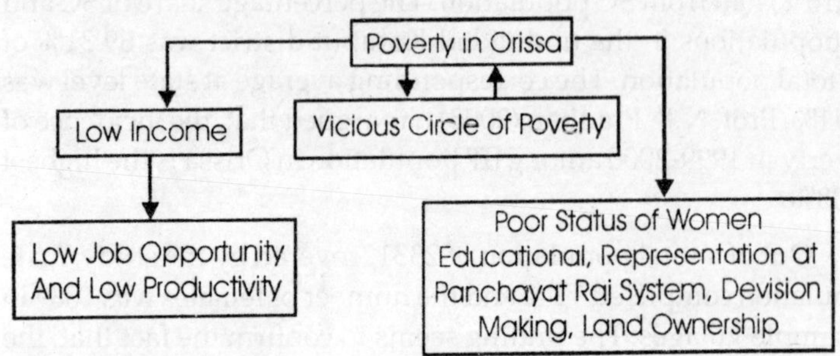

Educational Status of Women

A person's education can be important for getting a job and expansion in incomes. Education plays a positive role in the eradication of rural poverty and unemployment. It enhances the knowledge and skill of workers, the chance to enhance non-farm activities, helps better understanding and helps rational use of farm resource.

A glance at Table—1.1 depicts that the general literacy level of people of study area is 29.21% in 1987. The literacy level of female population is awfully low i.e. 12.03% and it lags far behind the literacy, performance of male persons that is 44.30%. The deplorable educational status of female population of the district is quite clear by perusal of their quality of education. Out of 131 literates upto primary, secondary and higher secondary educational levels worked out to 71, 40 and 19 respectively. Only one person was lucky enough to have degree certificate. It follows that study areas of Koraput are educationally backward, though they have a higher percentage of literacy (29.21%) than the district (16.13%). Planned economic development both, at state and district levels have succeeded in accelerating the literacy accomplishment of people of Koraput and Orissa to 47% to 36.30% and 63.61% respectively in 2001. Male literacy rate performance has claimed a some what higher place (47.58%) in social ladder in the district, while the female population are complacent with a modest average i.e. 24.81%. We have to cover miles ahead in our journey of education for all.

Reference may be made of tribal literacy, which occupied low place in the map of development. Due to non-availability of figures relating to tribal literacy from 2001 census, reliance is placed on 1991 census. It was estimated that the literacy among the tribal was estimated at 22.31 per cent, out of which male literacy is 34.44 per cent and female literacy was 10.21 per cent.

Income Earning Opportunities and Work Participation Rate

There is substance in the argument that the level of income at a point of time is the sine-qua-non of the level of well being and living of a person. A worker is actively engaged in income earning activities for 183 days in a year. A non-worker, on the other hand is not productively employed in income earning activities. Koraput district has preponderance of rural population because out of 979835 people, as high as 487735 comprised rural population and urban population was reckoned at 492100 in 2001.

An enquiry into Table—1.2 is deemed necessary to assess the role of female and male workers in the backward district. The arithmetic of table depict that the district has a staggeringly high proportion of workers 65.34% (1583 persons) and marginal proportion of non-workers 34.66% (808 persons) in 1987. Out of 1583 of non-workers, the number of male workers was 919 and 694 workers comprised female population. The number of female workers employed in cultivation, agriculture labour, transportation and construction was 403,143,0 and 22 respectively. 22 female workers were employed in construction, no worker from female population was engaged in mining and 12 female workers eked out living from manufacturing. The number of female workers depending on business, collection of minor Forest produce and services was sloted at 4,12 and 0 respectively.

Data analysis of 2001 census denotes that, the poverty-ridden district has a greater proportion of workers 48.46% than the state of Orissa 38.88%. There has been a sharp increases in the percentage of agricultural labourers in Koraput district from 27.70% in 1987 to 48.46% in 2001. It is apparent from empirical studies that, the average income of a male cultivator, per annum is (Table—1.3) Rs. 2345.19 as against the corresponding amount of Rs. 2,338.38 for a female cultivator. The stresses and strains of work of a female agricultural labourer fetch her Rs. 867.45 per annum far below the income of a male agricultural labourer that is Rs. 1031.12.

Table—1.2: Statement indicating age-wise and sex-wise composition of workers in study areas (1987-88)

Sl. No.	*Age-group Name of the Block*	*Male workers*	*Non-workers*	*Female workers*	*Non-workers*	*Total workers*	*Total non-workers*
1.	**Below 14 years**						
	Narayanpatna	3	84	–	108	3	192
	Kotpad	5	81	28	131	33	212
	Jeypore	24	90	52	83	76	173
	Total	32	255	30	322	112	577
2.	**15 years to 59 years**						
	Narayanpatna	232	–	182	–	414	–
	Kotpad	290	3	157	21	447	24
	Jeypore	356	14	182	87	538	101
	Total	878	17	521	108	1399	125
3.	**60 years and above 60 years**						
	Narayanpatna	–	4	–	3	–	7
	Kotpad	3	22	1	20	4	42
	Jeypore	6	25	2	32	8	57
	Total	9	51	3	55	12	106
	Grand total	**919 (60.34%)**	**323 (39.66%)**	**604 (39.66%)**	**485 (60.34%)**	**1523 (65.34%)**	**808 (34.66%)**

Source: (1) Sample survey, 1987-88.

(2) Mohapatro, P.C. and Patnaik, Eswar Rao, Women's participation in rural development. A case study of Narayanpatna block, *Indian Economic Journal* (Conference volume) No. 70th, 1987 (p. 201-202).

Presided by noble laureate Amartya Sen, Indian Economic Association, Rajasthan.

Table—1.3: Table unfolding sector-wise flow of income for different categories of workers in study area of Koraput (1987-88)

Sl. No.	Occupational break up	Narayan patna block workers				Kotpad Block workers				Jeypore Block workers				Grand Total	
		No. of males	Income in Rs.	No. of females	Income in Rs.	No. of males	Income in Rs.	No. of females	Income in Rs.	No. of males	Income in Rs.	No. of females	Income in Rs.	No. of male workers	No. of female workers
1.	Cultivators	106	211665	130	259590	142	420621	123	364341	228	484023	150	318437	476	403
2.	Agricultural labourers	56	45782	36	29430	61	64050	42	32160	64	76800	65	62456	181	145
3.	Transport	16	25885	-	-	19	23385	0	-	20	200796	0	-	55	-
4.	Construction	9	6000	6	3000	11	6600	7	3150	12	7200	9	4050	32	22
5.	Mining/Quarrying	16	9250	-	-	18	15456	0	-	20	24450	0	-	54	0
6.	Manufacturing	15	12750	4	1945	18	14400	5	1720	17	76500	3	6800	50	12
7.	Business	4	48000	2	15315	5	4500	3	17170	6	90000	3	32560	15	18
8.	(a) Forest collection	7	52500	4	16471	-	-	-	-	-	-	-	-	7	14
	(b) Livestock	0	-	0	-	6	6510	6	6510	7	11550	6	9118	13	12
9.	Services	6	35049	-	-	16	117576	0	-	14	293370	0	-	86	-
	Total	**235**	**446881** (Rs. 1902)	**182**	**325751** (Rs. 1790)	**296**	**713598** (Rs. 2411)	**186**	**425051** (Rs. 2285)	**388**	**1264639** (Rs. 3260)	**236**	**433421** (Rs. 1836)	**919** (60.34%)	**604** (39.66%)

Total No. of workers = 1523. * Aggregate Income Rs. 3609401. * Average: (Rs. 2370).

Average Income of Males Rs. 2639. * Average Income of Females of Rs. 1961.

Source: Tribal Problem in India, ed., Dr. S.N. Tripathy.

With regard to wages paid for agricultural labourer, it was flashed by field for agricultural labourer, it was flashed by field studies that, a male agricultural labourer was Rs. 6.00 per day. The lack of implementation of minimum wages Act and Equal Remuneration Act 1976 is a detterent on empowerment of women. The National sample survey has computed one woman unit of work equal to only one-half unit of a female labour. In the recent past, public action was directed to fix minimum wages Bhubaneswar and Cuttack, while the corresponding figure stood at Rs. 94.04 in other parts of the State.

SECTION–II

Factors like, small size of holdings, skewed land ownership, extreme drought conditions, employment of traditional antiquated and unproductive tools, equipments and implements, illiteracy, seasonal nature of employment in agriculture, lack of entrepreneurship, slender irrigation base of the economy (11.5%) seem to have accentuated the problem of rural poverty in the district.

While, the average size of land holding is 5.35 acres per cultivating household, the average size of family is staggering high (5.99 per household) in the region. In majority of cases, land records and titles to land ownership are in favour of male persons. The wheels of agricultural progress of Koraput economy are pushed backward because, the agrarian economy is dominated by marginal and small farmers, who comprise 37.71% and 28.28% of total cultivating households.

There is limited use of fertilisers (7.7 kgs. per hector), the impact of tractors and diesel pumps in limited to 4 households, and a priority input like irrigation claims a marginal proportion of total input outlay of the farmer 1.8%.

The history of agricultural development revolves more round development of food crops like paddy, wheat which claims roughly 71.25% of total cropped area. Although the district receives an average rainfall of 1521.8 mm, the actual rainfall recorded in 2000 was Koraput 1359 mm. The base of cropping intensity of economy is slender i.e. 134%. Analysts reason out that low productivity of crops is the probable explanation of low income of firm households. While the average yield per acre for paddy has marginally increased from 6.8 Qtls. In 1987 to 8.52 Qtls. in 1995-96, the per acre yield of Ragi shot up from 3.3 Qtls. in 1987-88 to 3.3 Qtls. in 1995-96. The area under HYV paddy has picked up from 23% in 1987 to 43% in 2000.

The impoverishment of women cultivators of the areas seems to be due to absence of lucrative prices for agricultural products. Recent facts and developments at Koraput and Jeypur region suggest that the peasants are unable to secure procurement price for paddy at the officially declared rate because the FCI do not purchase paddy from growers directly. The growers dispose of paddy to millers (who charge exorbitant commission for the services) at a price for below official prices. Grinding poverty of women in the agrarian economy stems from the fact that, agriculture is not a remunerative occupation. The gross income per acre of cultivated land in Koraput district was Rs.1299.40 while the net income worked out to be Rs. 921.20. The Koraput survey by Dr. P.C. Mohapatro 1977 has flashed that the net income and gross income per acre of cultivated land was Rs. 1499 and Rs. 299 in 1977-78 respectively. It follows that plan exercises have succeeded in increasing the net income accruing to agriculture by 6.53 times within a decade. Analysts argue that the minimum guaranteed prices announced prior to sowing season would go a long way in releasing surplus to market and iron out fluctuations in the market. It is possible that an increase in agricultural prices may induce progressive women farmers to assume risks in the adoption of new techniques with enhanced saving pool. It is plausible to believe that the procurement price of common paddy has picked up from 4.60 times from Rs. 105 per Qtl. in 1980-81 to Rs. 490 per Qtl. in 1999-2000.

The entitlements of rural women are not enforced because of exploitation by usurious money lenders who lend to farmers during the sowing season in form of paddy. It was understood that the farmers would repay double the amount of paddy after harvest (50% rate of interest on loan). LAMPS and Gramin Banks lend money but insist on security and lend primarily for production and not consumption lines. Tractors and money lenders cover their loan operations for production and consumption lines. It is deplorable that the women cultivators, quite like their male cultivators to sell their meagre surplus produce to traders and money lenders of the village at prices dictated by them. It is no eighth wonder, that sales operations by cultivators to lenders within the village results in distress sales.

Suggestions and Conclusions

There is a general impression that Koraput district has very high percentage of depressed population, low literacy level, poor health facility, poor banking facility, poor communication and transportation, poor rural electrification (Orissa Development Report 2004, Govt. of Orissa). The palpable deficiency of the social and economic infrastructure will retard women's earning capacity. A close look at the statistical abstract of Orissa 2002, would show that merely 54.26% of villages of Koraput are covered by electricity facilities in 2000-2001. The district has merely 43 Km. of roads per 100 Sq.Kms. area has not yet reached the all Orissa average of 15.03 Kms. area. Motor vehicle density per Sq. Km. land area was only 4.98. The railway route length per 1000 Sq.Km. area has not yet reached the all Orissa average 15.03 Km.. The district has to catch up the all Orissa average of 64.94 primary schools per lakh population. The per capita deposit of the peasant economy should shot up from the present low level of Rs. 253 to impressive level. The percentage of roads connected with all weather roads should touch the state average of 40%. The performance of Koraput economy in providing bank branches per lakh population is moderate i.e. 6.11.

The three fold strategy of education, health and employment (and agricultural development) has been rightly recognised by planners to raise the women in the socio-economic ladder of society. The programme of universalisation of elementary education and nutrition has to be suitably directed towards higher enrolment and retention of girls in schools. With a view to widening the base of work participation among females, focus may be laid on horticultural lines, dairying, palmgur processing, embroidery, needle work, goat and sheet rearing. Mid-day meals may be provided in schools to attract low income girls to continue their studies. In agriculture, plan endeavour may be directed towards scientific agriculture, irrigation, extension work, timely supply of seeds to needy people, shift in cropping pattern from food crops like paddy to commercial crops like mung, sugar cane, tobacco and coffee. Self Help Groups who came forward with viable schemes need encouragement from NABARD.

Table—1.4: The quality of human population as reflected in their literacy attainment in study areas

(M = Male, F = Female)

Name of the block	*Literates up to primary education*		*Literates up to secondary education*		*Literates up to higher secondary*		*Literates up to degree level*		*Grand total*		
	M	*F*	*M*	*F*	*M*	*F*	*M*	*F*	*M*	*Total*	*F*
1	*2*	*3*	*4*	*5*	*6*	*7*	*8*	*9*	*10*		*11*
Narayana Patna	62	11	39	11	15	0	Nil	0	116	(138)	22
Kotpad	47	16	30	9	70	4	5	0	152	(181)	29
Jeypore	100	44	80	20	82	15	20	1	282	(362)	80
Total	**209**	**71**	**149**	**40**	**167**	**19**	**25**	**1**	**550**	**(681)**	**131**

(Table Contd...)

Name of the Block	*Literacy rate at district level*	*Literacy rate at state level*	*Number of literacy in study areas*		*2001 census literacy rate Koraput*		*Total*
			M	*F*	*M*	*F*	
	12	13	14	15			
Narayana Patna			207	271			
Kotpad			252	329			
Jeypore			233	358			
					47.20%	24.26%	
Total	**16.13%**	**34.2%**	**692**	**958**	**(1650)**		

Literacy percentage: Male population = 44.28%

Female population = 12.03%

Source: 1. Sample survey, 1987-88.

2. Columns 12 & 13, Economic Survey, 1988, p. 12 to 20.

Note: Orissa literacy rate 2001 census, Male- 75.35%, Female- 50.51%, Total- 63.08%.

Table—1.5: Rough estimate of gross income and net income per acre of cultivated land for selected crops in Rs. in study pares of Koraput (1987-88)

Sl. No.	*Name of the crop*	*Total cultivated area*	*Total crop yield*	*Per acre yield*	*Price per Qtls.*
(1)	*(2)*	*(3)*	*(4)*	*(5)*	*(6)*
Cereals					
1.	Kharif paddy	1106.25	7528.910	6.80	198.010
2.	Rabi paddy	144.67	568.950	3.933	195.012
3.	Wheat	22.60	281.000	8.894	111.370
Mino Rnilet					
4.	Ragi	206.80	888.000	3.327	148.300
5.	Bazra	21.40	29.750	1.343	189.780
6.	Maize	1.00	1.000	1.000	100.000
Pulses					
7.	Biri (Black gram)	24.30	37.700	1.551	392.530
8.	Arhar	16.22	29.648	1.830	439.470
9.	Mung (Green gram)	28.54	46.200	1.620	405.540
10.	Horse gram	62.80	182.748	2.910	243.310
Oil seeds					
11.	Til	6.70	8.200	1.223	347.000
12.	Nigri	20.85	21.890	1.050	350.340
13.	Caster	6.20	11.600	1.871	619.000
14.	Soyabean	17.00	54.000	3.176	300.000

(Table Contd...)

(1)	(2)	(3)	(4)	(5)	(6)
Other crops					
15.	Sugar cane	15.00	225 Tonnes	15 Tonnes	200 per tonnes
16.	Tobacco	18.96	113.000	5.960	970.000
Vegetable					
17.	Onions	4.71	28.630	6.078	449.967
18.	Tomatoes	1.00	2.000	2.000	1.000
19.	Brinjals	4.00	60.150	15.037	224.440
	Total	**1584.33 Acres**			

(Table Contd...)

Sl. No.	Name of the crop	Total gross income (in Rs.)	Gross income per acre (in Rs.) (col. 4 × 6)	Gross input in Rs. (col. 5 × 6)	Average gross in out per acre in Rs. (col. 9/3)	Net income in rupees per acre (col. 8-10)
(7)	(8)	(9)	(10)	(11)	(12)	(13)
Cereals						
1.	Kharif paddy	1490621.200	1340.47	407100.000	368.000	978.97
2.	Rabi paddy	112659.100	778.782	69152.26	478.000	300.78
3.	Wheat	42485.370	1879.925	11294.100	499.740	1389.19
Mino Rnilet						
4.	Ragi	102071.680	493.593	24026.651	116.184	377.41
5.	Bazra	5456.175	254.074	1110.000	51.874	203.00
6.	Maize	100.000	100.000	10.000	10.000	90.00
Pulses						
7.	Biri (Black gram)	14798.300	608.614	5875.700	209.000	399.81
8.	Arhar	12139.978	749.330	2298.000	141.183	608.15
9.	Mung (Green gram)	18782.150	658.595	6943.890	243.270	415.32
10.	Horse gram	44454.15	708.032	7765.848	123.660	580.37

(Table Contd...)

(7)	(8)	(9)	(10)	(11)	(12)	(13)
Oil seeds						
11.	Til	2845.40	424.360	836.670	123.030	300.50
12.	Nigri	7679.890	360.0382	2153.930	103.308	264.13
13.	Caster	7180.400	1158.150	632.400	102.000	1056.15
14.	Soyabean	16200.000	552.800	3900.000	229.410	723.35
Other crops						
15.	Sugar cane	45000.000	3000.000	18000.000	1200.000	1800.00
16.	Tobacco	109610.000	5781.200	29899.000	1576.950	4204.250
Vegetable						
17.	Onions	12882.550	2734.800	4798.000	1018.680	1715.21
18.	Tomatoes	200.000	200.000	65.000	65.000	135.00
19.	Brinjals	13500.000	3374.900	4001.000	1000.250	2374.65
	Total	**Rs. 2058676.10**		**Rs. 5990**		

Source: Sample survey, 1987-88.

Good health enhances productivity and earning capacity of female workers. To improve the working capabilities of women and to reduce female mortality in the district the existing hospitals should have sufficient physicians, lady doctors, nurses, ayahs and medical beds. Humanitarian doctors responsive to peoples' needs should come forward to wipe out tears from every eye.

To conclude, it is high time that an integrated approach was adopted for the overall development of women fold to enable them to participate in the socio-economic and cultural development of our country. The problem of women's development should constitute an important segment of women's development. Any further neglect of this important issue would stand in the way of economic development of the country.

REFERENCES

1. Statistical Abstract of Orissa, 2002.
2. *Economic Survey*, 2001-02, Govt. of Orissa.
3. *Yojana*, May 1988.
4. Plan Documents, Govt. of Orissa.
5. Thesis of Pattnayak, E.R., "*The Problems and Prospects of Agricultural Development during Sixth Five Year Plan in Koraput District*".
6. Mohapatro, P.C. and Pattnayak, E.R. "Make them Equal Partnership in Development", *Yojana*, May 1988.
7. Padhisharma, Prof. R "Role of Tribal in Economic Development of Orissa", *Orissa Economic Journal*, 2003.
8. Chattopadhya, A., "Women and Entrepreneurship", *Yojana*, January 2005.

2

Empowerment of Indian Women

A Challenge for 21st Century

Dr. Dasarathi Bhuyan

Women's empowerment is a new phrase in the vocabulary of gender literature. The phrase is used in two broad senses i.e. general and specific. In a general sense, it refers to empowering women to be self-dependent by providing them access to all these freedoms and opportunities, which they were denied in the past only because of their being a 'women'. In a specific sense, women empowerment refers to enhancing their position in the power structure of the society.

The word women empowerment essentially means that the women have the power or capacity to regulate their day-to-day lives in the social, political and economic terms—a power which enables them to move from the periphery to the centre stage.

The principle of gender equality is enshrined in the India constitution in its preamble, fundamental rights, fundamental duties and directive principles. The constitution not only grants equality to women but also empowers the state to adopt measures a position discrimination infavour of women. Within the framework of democratic polity, our laws, developmental policies, plans and programmes have aimed at women's advancement in different spheres. India has also ratified various international conventions to secure rights of women. The women's movement and a widespread network of Non-Government Organisations (NGOs) having strong grass-root presence and deep insight into women's concerns have contributed in inspiring initiatives for the empowerment of women. Women today trying to understand their position in society. Women have become increasingly aware of sexual inequalities in every sphere of life and are seeking ways to fight them.

The Indian women has cast of their age-old shackles of serfdom and male domination. She has come to her own and started scaling the ladders of social advance with proud and dignity. Women of India are now uplifted and emancipated and granted equal status with men in all walks of life—political, economic, social, domestic and educational. They have a franchise, they are free to join any service or follow any profession. Free India has, besides her woman prime minister, women ambassadors, women cabinet ministers, women legislators, women governors, women scientists-engineers-doctors-space researchers-giant IT specialists, women Generals, women public officers, judiciary officers and in many more responsible positions. No distinction is now made in matters of education between boys and girls. Their voice is now as forceful and important as that of men. They are becoming equal partners in making or dismissing of a government.

Hindu law has been changed and modified. Far-reaching changes have been introduced in the Hindu Marriage Act. Women have been given right to divorce in certain cases. Besides this, the Hindu Succession Act has given to the daughter; the right to the property of her parents. Our constitution has given equal rights to women. No distinction has been made on the basis of caste, religion or sex. Their rights have thus been safeguarded. Thirdly, three per cent reservation for women is apt to be enacted in her future.

Women Empowerment—Still An Illusion of Reality

Not-with-standing the remarkable changes in the position of women in free India, there is still a great divergence between the constitutional position and stark reality of deprivation and degradation. Whatever whiff of emancipation has blown in Indian society, has been inhaled and enjoyed by the women belonging to the rural areas are still totally untouched by the winds of change. They still have been living in miserable conditions, steeped in poverty, ignorance, superstition and slavery. There still exists a wide gulf between the goals enunciated in the constitution, legislations, policies, plans, programmes and related mechanisms on the one hand and the situational reality of the status of women in India, on the other. The human rights scenario in the country continues to be dismal and depressing. Women are being brutalised, commodified, materialised and subjected to inhuman exploitation and discrimination.

Although, gender discrimination has been banned by the constitution and women have been guaranteed political equality with men, yet there is a difference between the constitutional rights and the rights enjoyed in reality by women. Even after half a century of independence, barring a few exceptions, women have remained outside the domain of power and political authority. Although they constitute about half of the citizen, over the years their participation by way of voting has increased, yet their participation and representation in law making and law implementing bodies are not very satisfactory. No doubt the 73rd and 74th constitutional amendment acts have provided access to women in the decision making process at the grass-root level but their representation in the parliament and state legislatures is woefully poor. Insecurity does not allow the women leaders to identify leadership at the grass-root level. In politics when a man proposes, they themselves despose. In reality women representatives are ornamental in nature and political consciousness is found lacking among them .They are affected by the caste and class divisions, feudal attitudes, patriarchal nature of the family and village social, environmental, ethnic, religious separatism and the like. They are members on record only. Allegedly, they are not consulted while taking decision. Thus women representatives are not free from male dominance in the village administration and no significance change in the power equal is observed in the villages.

In these days of scam-ridden politics, the increasing role of money and mafia in elections keeps most of the women away from politics. Increasing violence and vulgarity against them intimates women and consequently they prefer to stay out of politics.

What are the reasons for this sorry state of affairs? Issues may be various and varied however a few basic issues deserve specific mention:

- Lack of awareness;
- Lack of social and economic empowerment;
- Lack of political will;
- Feebleness of accountability mechanisms;
- Lack of enforcement by the police force;
- Lack of gender culture.

The question arises, how greater participation of women in politics can be achieved? Generally, the answer is suggested in the form of 'reservation'. However, mere reservation will not solve the problem unless and until women are given commensurate powers to function effectively and they themselves become more conscious and aware of their rights and duties.

More Steps to be Taken

There can not any dramatic movement in the system just by including women members in Grampanchayat. At the same time, it is also essential to shed certain stereotyped prevailing notions about role and importance of women in socio-economic development. Women should be encouraged to play a more active part. The male representatives have to establish a rapport with female representatives and give due respect and attention to their views. In the process of development and decision making women have to operate along with men.

Of course, there is some awareness among women due to reservation for them in the Panchayati Raj Institutions (PRIs). But there is need for appropriate training and education relating to different aspects of in functioning of panchayats to make women members conscious enough of their effective role and representation in the Panchayat Samity. This kind of training can be organised at the district or block level immediately following the election. We have to understand that women representatives can play a vital role in the formulation and implementation of various women and child development programmes. This would increase the efficacy of such programmes. For instance, the women representatives and Gram Panchayat should have sufficient control over the primary education, primary health care and running of the public distribution system.

The state must pass and enforce legislations so that the status of women in society is brought to a respectable level through the long arms of the law. In 1985, a separate department of women and child development (WCD) was set up. In the Sixth Five Year Plan, a separate chapter on "Women and Development" was included. The government had started and implemented major programmes like Support to Training-cum-Employment for Women (STEP), Mahilakosh, Women's Development Corporation, etc. However, legislations and efforts of the state have not made deeper in roads into the rural and urban areas. For example, sex determination of foetus still continues in all the rural regions of the country despite the enforcement of legislation on Pre-natal Diagnostic Technique (Regulation and Prevention of Misuse) Act, which was passed in 1994. The women of India must oppose this sex determination of foetus, eve-teasing, bride burning, child marriages, exploitation in the offices, lower wages for labour, etc., women from all walks of life must unite and must give priority to their education, growth and the prosperity of their families. Police should accept more female officers and constable so that they are able to tackle with the female victims of our society. Female infanticide, female torture, sati and dowry must be banned in the country.

Women must become literate, as education is beneficial for them as well as their families. The family web is woven around the women. She has to be up to the mark and educated so that she could fend for herself and her family during the hour of crisis. The status of women would improve only if they education themselves and grab every opportunity to become stronger and more powerful than before.

The discussion brings a major conclusion to light-the status of women could be improved by women themselves and nobody else. It is the modern era of satellites, achievements and technology-based gadget. Why should women be left behind?

There should be a better and fuller understanding of the problems peculiar to woman, to make a solution of those problems possible. As these problems centre round the basic problem of inequality, steps should be taken to promote equality of treatment and full integration of woman in the total development effects of the country.

The main stress should be on equal work and elimination of discrimination in employment. One of the basic policy objectives should be universal education of woman, the lack of which tends to perpetuate the unequal status quo. The popular UNESCO slogan should come in handy: "*educate a man and you educate an individual; educate a woman and you educate a family*."

Women will have to empower themselves 'from below' in order to compel the government to empower them 'from above'. Further, there is a need for a change of values and behaviour in the society, a need for positive socio-cultural and economic empowerment and above all the will power and strong determination of women to join politics. Education can play a vital role in bringing about the desirable behavioural changes among the women and make them well equipped in terms of knowledge, competence and capacity to deal with different political problems.

It may be concluded that women have shifted traditional assumptions about their roles and capabilities. There has been a marked change, and it has been for the better. Many of its benefits however have yet to touch the majority and all of us continue to experience forms of gender discrimination. If laws designed to address the concerns of women are to have a dramatic and positive impact on woman's lives, they must be sensitive to the social, economic and political disempowerment of women throughout the world. The most important measure of their success should be the extent to which they enable woman to interpret, apply and enforce laws of their own making, incorporating their own voices, values and concerns.

3

Women Empowerment

Dynamics and Dimensions

Dr. Nilanchal Muni

While nature has made men and women differently, society and culture determine the roles that they perform and the value accorded to each. Their status therefore depends on the attitudes of the society towards men and women according to the various roles they play at home and in society. For centuries, women have been relegated to a secondary status in the family and the society. For Thus in true of all societies across the world and is not a modern phenomenon. It is as old as civilisation it self. Even in very old times when communities were not so well demarcated and were considered primitive men would be hunters and women were responsible for looking after the children and family. The role of 'hunting' performed by men was given higher value (status) then the role of 'looking after the children' performed by women. As civilisation advanced the women got identified with roles related to the home or the 'private sphere' and the men with those roles related to productive work outside the home or the 'public' sphere.

In the modern days, when women have started performing multiple roles of working in and outside the home and much greater equality is accorded to them, they still not completely equal. The fundamental basis for this inequality is the unequal access to economic, social and political opportunities between men and women. It is also said that this difference in role was determined not by the biological differences between men and women, in other words by the sex of the individual but by the gender of the individual.

What is Women's Empowerment

The term empowerment is frequently heard today, whether in the media or in the class room. It is clearly connected to the word "power". Simply speaking empowerment is derived from the word 'empower' meaning to give or to acquire power or to increase power. Thus the word empowerment also implies a change in the equation or level of power. It can therefore be viewed as both a process as well as a result of social change.

The term "power" in turn connotes control. In the context of human society, it means control over resources. These resources include natural resources, financial resources, human resources, intellectual resources, etc. Power is relational dynamic between individual or between groups, unequally distributed.

Srilata Batliwala,. a well known woman activist has defined women's empowerment as the "process by which women gain greater control over material and intellectual resources and the gender based discrimination against women in all institutions and structures of society" women empowerment is the process by which women negotiate a more equitable distribution of power, a greater space in the initial decision making process in the home, in the community and in economic and political life.

Dimensions of Women's Empowerment

The empowerment question needs to be addressed with in the larger context of development we need to ask why empowerment ? And while empowerment is not synonymous with development, the process of empowerment implies broader, systematic change in the way society is structured. And in that sense, empowerment is a necessary part and parcel of any genuine development effort that seeks to ultimately empower the disempowered.

At the overall level women's empowerment aims at changing the balance of power between the sexes so as to create a more equitable distribution of power in society. However, when we examine this overall process of women's empowerment more closely we become aware of the economic, social, political and legal dimensions of the process. Each of these dimensions is interlinked to the other and have a bearing on each other.

"Economic empowerment" implies a better quality of material life through sustainable livelihood owned and managed by women.

By "social empowerment" we mean a more equitable social status for women in society.

"Legal empowerment" is the provision of an effective legal structure which is supportive of women's empowerment.

"Political empowerment" through struggle and movement based work are important preconditions for economic empowerment.

Development workers at the grassroots level have debated for long on what kind of empowerment should take place first—economic, social or political . Women at the grassroots have been heard saying they must first have food, a full stomach for the whole family and only then would they be able to discuss empowerment. Yet other development workers believe social and political empowerment through struggle and movement based work are important preconditions for economic empowerment.

Yet another concern among many is whether the empowerment of women aimed against men while it is true that there may be some confusion on this score the apprehension that the empowerment of women will go against the interest of men or that it well disempowered men is not true. Empowerment of women is against patriarchy and its control and not against men. The aim of greater empowerment of women is the fuller and wholesome development of both men and women. Freeing women from the fetters of the past and of stereotyped sex roles will also free men from the boundaries of their traditional roles and behavioural patterns. The idea is to provide both men and women with opportunities for their equal development. The liberation of men may mean they have to let go of their traditional rights and power over women and they may want to have a relationship with women which may want to have a relationship with women which may want to have a relationship with women which rests on mutual respect for each others rights and responsibilities.

Changes in law pertaining to marriage, property, sexual harassment, dowry, rape and other forms of violence, so as to bring in laws favouring or supporting women's empowerment are necessary, but not enough progressive laws do provide a good environment for women's empowerment, but the provision of law on itself is only the first step. Enabling women to actually access the benefits of appropriate laws is the key task of the empowerment process.

Further, disempowerment effects women from different strata of society differently women living in poverty carry a double burden. They have to bottle with ravages and challenges of poverty as well as the fight for greater gender equity.

The empowerment of women is thus encompassing process that seeks to transform the society. Change is needed in the economic, social and political dimensions of life for the success of the empowerment process.

Indicators of Women's Empowerment

Indicators of women empowerment are the measurable changes that occur in the position and status of women. Identifying the indicators of the empowerment process is a complex task. Much depends on who is examining this subject, and at what point of time. It would however be fair to say that women who are engaged in the process of empowering themselves are in the best position to decide such indicators. In such a case the indicators would be based on the actual life experiences of the women. Some examples of the indicators of women's empowerment are—change in women's self-perception from negative to positive, increase in self-esteem and self confidence, clear increase in level in her capacity to take decision independently and the development of her ability to speak out and to defend herself against the violations of her human rights.

Empowering Process

The process of empowerment which seeks an equitable and active share of power for women, has to deal with the burden of ideas and values which are passed on to women as part of their socialisation process from their very childhood. This social condition becomes part of her person and her mind set process therefore must begin with women changing their own ways of thinking and behaving. This means , first and foremost, women's consciousness has to be changed.

Women have to change the way they look at themselves. There must be an increase in their self-esteem, in their self-confidence and in their understanding of their own strength and potential. Their thinking and behaviour must evolve to become more independent. They must try to appreciate themselves more and to recognise and value their knowledge and skills and their contribution of the sustainability of the households and the community. They must realise the importance of asserting their basic rights. So the road to empowerment is a long, lonely and often frightening. But the struggle begins at the individual level and empowerment is a result of the struggle. In fact, the 'struggle' is the process of empowerment.

In recent decades, while individual women have been alone. Women within communities, within countries and across the globe have been linking with one another to expand and to sharpen their efforts for their own empowerment. This trend is reflected in the emergence of hundreds of women's organisation be they Non-Government Organisations (NGOs) or cooperatives or banking or trade unions or large federations of women's organisation or mass based social movements of women. Thus the individual struggle sustained by collective efforts and the reverse is also true.

Who Empowers

There are no one person or institution or agency, which alone empowers women. The creation of an enabling environment through strong polity support, the work of voluntary organisation, women's group, academicians and researchers, committed bureaucrats and other support groups are among the multitude of agents who can provide support to take forward the agenda of women empowerment. And yet, ultimately it is the women herself who has to empower herself within the family and outside the home. The others can only facilitate the process of empowerment. All the external agents or forces can only facilitate the process of empowerment organising and empowering women at the grassroots in rural and urban areas has now become a key task of field based development workers. The mobilisation of women to form Self Help

Groups (SHGs) is a widely popular method of organising and empowering them. SHGs bring together underprivileged women from a common socio-economic background. It then helps poor women to meet regular to discuss about common problems and to work together for their collective empowerment. Mature SHGs also help to develop local women leaders who can contribute to the development of the entire village community.

There are clear advantage of the collective approach to women's empowerment since no one single women alone has to face the obstacles that may arise. Further, SHGs allows women to pool together their material (savings) and human resources reduces individual risk and promotes democratic ways of working SHGs can also serve as a voice for negotiating access to various resources for women struggling to overcome their class and gender oppression.

However, the empowerment process takes place in the lager social and political environment in which women live. This large context both supports and hinders the empowerment process. The influential leaders, institutions, policy and laws which are part of the larger environment must provide continuing support. And the movement for empowerment must in turn advocate and lobby for the transformation of the key elements which form the environment.

There are some women organisations which have been playing a dynamic role for women empowerment. The first of its kind SEWA (Self Employed Women's Association), Ahmedabad. This is an organisation made up poor self-employed women such as vegetable and other vendors, milk maids, garment workers, agarbati workers, etc. It has helped top organise their own trade union to fight for better wages and labour rights.

The Annapurna Mahila Mandal, located in Mumbai is a large Credit Cooperative Soviety of the poor women. The Mandal provide small amount and short term loans to its members to start their business at home. The Mandal also works for the defence of women's economic, legal and human rights.

There are yet other large women's organisations which are part of the micro credit movement. The better known among such organisations which help women access cheap and ready credit are Friend and Women World Banking Community Development Fund, Hyderabad and Working Women's Forum, Chennai.

Another organisation working in the tribal belt of eastern Gujarat is DISHA (Development Initiative for Social and Human Action). DISHA has helped to organise thousands of tribal women to protect their rights. These women are mostly forest workers or minor forest produce collectors or daily wage workers.

Conclusions

The process of women empowerment begins when women's awareness must be accompanied by or followed by more education, greater knowledge and useful skills and action. When women organise for action they gain further knowledge and their awareness is raised to a new level. This increased awareness leads to new action and the whole process is repeated. Such a continuous process can lead to higher level of empowerment. The greater and greater change that may follow can change the very belief or assumption of what constitute power. Action brings about higher level of consciousness and greater consciousness in turn leads to more effective action. Collective action through organising for women's empowerment such as through SHGs introduces an element of democratic decision making leads to the development of leadership. Reduces risk and external threat and enables women to overcome the oppression of patriarchy and to realise their own true potential and worth.

4

Women Empowerment

A Historical Perspective

Subhrabala Behera

The movement for the empowerment of women is a major part of human civilization. It has been of the significant social and political development of the closing decades of the 20th century. Women constitute almost half of the population have subjected to the tyranny and oppression of a particular order for centuries and in fact even today. Today among various issues, gender has gained primacy in recent discourses on social analysis because of its spread and effect. Gender inequality is pervasive in various layers of social existence as its tentacles are spread across various segments of society.

UN observed the year 1975 as the international women's year. This indicates that the UN has convinced that the state of women throughout the world was not good. Therefore, UN wanted to draw particular attention of the whole world to the unsatisfactory condition of women as a whole. To give more importance to the women, 8th March is now observed as the International Women's Day. To improve the conditions of women to provide rights. Privileges and justice to the women are the main objectives of international women's day. It is also known as women empowerment day.

Empowerment of women implies process by which women's power of self-realisation is promoted and reinforced. They develop the capacity for self-reliance out crossing the relationship subordination on account of gender, social and economic status and the role in the family and society. It encompasses the ability to make choices, control resources and enjoy participatory relationship within family and community. To achieve these objectives empowerment of women also implies their ability to participate in it and also lead social movements to remove obstacles in their progress towards their goal.

If we visualise the state and status of women in India from the ancient period till the modern age we will find that the position of women changes from period to period. In ancient period women enjoyed a high position and equal status with the men. They also worshipped by the society. But in the middle age this attitude came to change. In this period the position of the women was very sufferable and worst. Several restrictions were imposed on them. But, during British regime, some radical changes taken place in the sphere of education, life, etc. After independence several programmes and remedial measures are taken to develop and uplift women.

From the day of Adam and Eve, women have been treated as the second sex. The western world has viewed women either in the image of Eve or in the image of Mary. India there has been too, stereo typical glorification of the women. History tells us that Indian women enjoyed privileges positions in the society of vedic age. The Vedas glorified women as the mother, the creator one who gives life and worshipped her as 'devi' or goddess. Manu Samhita says that God feels joy where women are honoured. Really, women were given honoured by the people.

But, this position of women in society did not continue in the muslim period. Suppression of women increased manifold. Sati, child marriage, the devadasi system, purdah system, dowry, polyandry, polygamy and female infanticide, etc. were common during these times. Women's life was miserable. They only compelled to be satisfied with household affairs. They were not given education and opportunities to participate in the activities of men. She was considered a 'parayadhan' in her own materials home.

During the British rule, things began to change for the better. Because British introduced English education in India. Some important and prominent person of the age thought that women should be educated equally like men and every opportunity should be provided to them. It was the influence of English education on some prominent persons. So women were given English education. But Indians were very ignorant, conservative, superstitious and illiterate. Therefore, the progress work very slow at the out set. Gradually, the mental outlook of the men changed and they wanted for women's education and opportunity. Schools and colleges were established and education began to spread. In the Indian freedom struggle the women came to the fore front and helped in the women. All ignorant practices were abolished. The continually efforts of social reformer R.R.M. Ray, I.C. Bidyasagar etc. get success. Women's attempt of defining their role in the society started several women's movement in India. Bharat Stree Maha Mandal started first in Hydrabad (1910) then in Lahore, Delhi, Karachi, Allahabad, Kanpur, Hazaribad, Midnapur and Kalkotta for this purpose. Many other women like Sabitri Bai Phule, Pandit Rama Bai, Begum Ruzya, Sakhrid, Subhalaxmi etc. started school for girls. Some other started publication to highlight issues on women. Between 1917 to 1927 three Women's Association namely: Women's Indian Association, National Council of Women in India and All India Women's Conference were formed. A. Besanta, S. Naidu, Sister Nivedita and others formed allegation and met in Delhi demanding voting rights of women. The International Women's Council had a National chapter for the states of women purpose. All India Women's Conference (AIWC) which still exists was formed for this purpose.

After independence Indian women attend the bonafide citizenship of the new nation. All the framers of the Constitution agreed on the basic principles of equality, rights and privileges, yet they expressed divergent views when it was apply to the traditional strong hold of male privileges viz. right property and overall predominance in the family. However, it was felt that women should be assigned on equal status with men on grounds of justice, growth and steps for transforming. The Preamble in Indian Constitution undertakes to secure all citizens, justice, social, economic, political, liberty of thought and worship, equality of status and opportunities and to promote fraternity among all and to promote dignity of the individual and unity of the nation.

Several acts were framed for the betterment of women. The Employees State Insurance Act 1948 provides benefit of sickness, maternity, disablement, dependencies, medical and funeral. The Factories Act 1948, The Mines Act 1952 and the Plantation Labour Act 1970, the Payment of Gratuity Act 1970 were made for the women ablement. Severasl provisions made in the Criminal Procedure Code, the Hindu Marriage Act, the Hindu Adoption and Maintenance Act provide special protection to men. The Directive Principle of State Policy Article 39 of the constitution embodies ideas that the state shall secure (equal pay for equal work) and ensure educate means of livelihood for both men and women. During the international women's year 1975, the Govt. of India promulgated equal remuneration ordinance.

After independence, many militant movements rise against the government like those led by Muni Memthala Renu Chakravarthy, Godavary Perullakar. Even in the Naxal movement in Bihar, Bengal, Arunachal Pradesh and Orissa, women were active. The Namiraman movement of Gujarat, SEWA, the Shabahada movement and the anti-price agitation are other levels of people struggle in which women provides leadership and actively participated. The first feminist organisations started in India were Stree Mukti Sangathan in Bombay, Purogamin Stree Sangathan (1991) in Pune, Socialist Women's Group and Stree Sangathan in Delhi and the Progressive Organisation in Hyderabad. They raise voice against oppression and exploitation of women, sexual harassment, rape, domestic violence, purdah, succession rights, divorce, personal laws, dowry torture and dowry deaths, beauty contests, prostitution, etc. Several activities are carried through workshops, conferences, demonstrations, public meetings, etc.

Thus, women today becomes equal with men. They become more skilled and successful in all fields. She is being viewed as an independent creature with a will, wish and feeling and a separate identity of her own. India has produced exemplary women who have contributions in the different fields. K. Bedi, P.T. Usha, Bachendri Pal, Kalpana Chawla, Arundhati Roy, S. Sen, Lata Dutt, Y. Kookhey, Lara Dutt, etc. have earned a name for themselves. Mrs. Vijayalaxmi Pandit became an ambassador and president of the UN among the women who is now Prime Minister, Governors of the States, Chief Ministers, Ministers, IAS officers, High Court-Supreme Court and other court judges and judicial officers, lawyers, doctors, professors, engineers, teachers, scientists, pilots, giant IT specialists and developers, eminent social workers, etc.

Besides, these government has created effective institutional frameworks to strengthen the movement for women empowerment. The status of women can also be viewed from a development perspective. Development as defined by the world conference of UN decade for women is interpreted to mean total development including political, social, economic, cultural, ethical, spiritual, physical, moral, intellectual and other dimensions. Likewise the 73rd and 74th Constitutional Amendment ensure 1/3rd of total seats for women in all elected offices including local bodies in both rural and urban areas for the advancement of women. Besides this, 33% reservation for women in legislature is provided by the government. The women of today is not merely a slave at home and of her husband. She has been playing a constructive role in the development of the society.

Yet, women has not achieved total emancipation. Now too women are poorly presented in the ranks of power, policy and decision making. Women make up less than 5% of the world's heads of the state, heads of major corporations and top position of international organisations. Still they are not free from exploitation, sexual harassment, untouchables, etc. The discrepancy in the ideology and practice of the empowerment policy of women in India constitutes its continual social, economic and cultural backwardness.

Another thing is that women should be conscious about their life, rights, privileges, status, position, etc. They must be careful about themselves. Men should realise about status and contribution of the women for the development of the society and they will give all the facilities and opportunities for their all round upliftment. The consciousness and mutual efforts of both men, women and society will lead to the empowerment of the women.

5

Globalisation and Its Impact on Women Empowerment

Dr. Bandana Gaur

The beginning of 21st century has come with greater turbulence and lesser stability in every sphere of social life. In all countries of the world changes in socio-economic and political environment are taking place rapidly with the introduction of the globalisation. In the context of women, it should supposedly elevate the socio-economic status of women. In the developed countries it is deemed that women have already achieved a high socio-economic status, but in the developing and the least developed countries they are lagging behind.

For centuries, women in India are suffering due to discrimination, exploitation and exposed to various kinds of harassment at various levels. Women constitute nearly half of total population of the country and therefore the development of the country is not possible without the development of this vast segment after independence there are various constitutional provisions to protect the interests of the women and undertaken various socio-economic development measures for their upliftment. In addition various voluntary organisations are also working hard for emancipation of women.

Empowerment of women conceptually forms distinct category by itself. It implies processes by which women's power of self organisation is promoted and reinforces, they develop the capacity for self-reliance out-crossing the relationship of subordinations on account of gender, social and economic status and the role in the family and society. It encompasses their ability to make choice control resources and enjoy participatory relationship within family and community.

Empowerment means the process by which people take control action to overcome obstacles. Empowerment especially refers to the collective action by the deprived and oppressed to overcome the obstacles of structural inequality which previously caused their disadvantaged position. It is a continuous and multi-dimensional process by which women are able to realise their potential and overcome obstacles.

The parameters of empowerment are developing the ability to think, critically building self-confidence, building up the group cohesion and fostering decision making and action ensuring effective participation on social change encouraging group action and providing infrastructure and climate for transformation. By empowerment women would be able to develop self-esteem, confidence, realise their potential and enhance their collective bargaining power.

The movement for the empowerment of women and its ideology has undergone significant differentiations in India since the time of the national movement, which was the first systematic effort in our country to bring women in the foreground of the national level participation in the activities of social, economic and political regeneration of society. This movement threw up a leadership among the women and also deeply influenced their role perception over the following decades commensurate with these objectives many legislative changes were introduced. The establishment of a national commission to monitor the status of women, reservation of 33 per cent of seats in the village panchayats (Councils) through a constitutional amendment and the measures being contemplated to reserve 33 per cent of seats for women in parliament and the state assembly testify to the increasing recognisation of the role of women in the power structure of our society.

Studies of empowerment of women all over the world have revealed that the efforts towards their empowerment succeeds only when attention is invited by women to their self-managed and self-sustained organisation and movement oriented activities and not when the agenda for the empowerment is made a part of the general development plan of society.

It is revealed that during the past decades sex ratio in the country has been continuously worsening. The illiteracy among women is endemic being 36 per cent compared to 64.3 per cent among women. With the exception of Kerala where the female literacy is 86.9 per cent, in states like Bihar, Rajasthan, Uttar Pradesh and Madhya Pradesh less than 30 per cent women are literate. whereas almost three-fourth of our population is concentrated in this region. The report prepared by the United National Development Programme (UNDP) places India at 103 out of 174 in the rank of "gender related development index". On "gender empowerment measure", India ranks 93 while China ranks 29, Indonesia 61 and its neighbour Nepal and Bhutan score better. Literacy is the most effective instrument of self-empowerment. If a society denies this right to most of its women, all its other claims towards taking steps for the empowerment of a women are easily nullified.

This discrepancy in the ideology and practice of the empowerment policy of women in our country constitutes the foundation of India's continued social, economic and cultural backwardness. It tells aversely upon effective implementation of the policies on population, health, child care and ecology development. These, as we know, are the building blocks of social and economic growth and modernisation of society. Deprivation of a women reinforces the social and cultural prejudices on gender issues in society. The female child is often denied the basic right to survival and most female children are given a second class status in terms of human rights. The empowerment of women in a society is most effective index of measuring modernisation and development. In India, we have to traverse a long distance to achieve the goal.

Globalisation for an Indian women could have been interpreted as amelioration of women's status, decline in her fertility obligations, a reduction in her mortality and contraception burdens, her empowerment for that he could overcome her predicaments, and her active participation in all the democratic institutions of society to ensure equity and justice. Globalisation further helps to feminise their poverty by bringing them to the level of poorest among the poor. They are victims of social neglect and crime, suffer life-long injustices, inequities and discrimination. Their standing in the globalised society will further deepen their miseries.

Now the time has come for women to come out of the dominance of man and to develop their own skills, to think, to work, to take decisions, independently. This will put the women in the top of the system in which they participate. It is a well known fact that some manufacturing companies, financial companies are being headed by women and are being managed comparatively better than the man.

Merely raising the issue understanding the present process of globalisation is not enough. The women's movement needs to face all these and other challenges. Therefore, the need of the hour is to create an environment, which ensure dignity to the women.

REFERENCES

1. Dr. Das, Rani Sandhya—*Empowerment of Women*, Third Concept, An International Journal of Ideas.
2. Gawari, Rita and Singh, Reena—*Globalisation and Women: Some Demographic Issues*. Globalisation, Culture and Women's Development.
3. Singh, Yogendra—*Globalisation and Social Change, Social Change.*

6

An Insight into Women Empowerment

The Indian Panorama

Smt. Anjail Dash*

8th March, the International Women's Day comes and passes off quietly with little jubilation on those long stretches of pale and remorseful faces meekly hung on the womanly frames. But much fanfare in created in seminars, workshops where pundits vehemently address the flamboyant issue of 'Women Empowerment'.

This has been happening ever since the coining of the term 'Women Empowerment'. Although this concept in its new robes has come to India through an accidental motion, its oriental origin is well traced into the Epic age. Seeta the finest women character exalted in all perfections eternally epitomizes chastity, forbearance and dignity. Still she was put to the dreadful and deadliest trials (twice) at the altar of fire to testify 'chastity' at the behest of her godly husband—Maryada Purushottam Raja Ram. And, legend holds it; woman dignity was beatified by the bold decision of this hitherto docile wife Seeta preferring self-immersion into the solacing lap of mother Earth, rather than going back to matrimony with her Raja Chakravarthy husband. The serene suffering of Seeta is aptly crept into the emergence of a fiery image of self-esteem in the form of

* **Senior Faculty (Management Studies), Department of Economics, College of Business Administration (CBA), Berhampur–760 010, (Orissa).**

Draupadee, the bold wife to five Pandavas. She reminds us of 'revenge' not 'penance' as the panacea for outraging the modesty of a woman in the Raj Sabha. Her tale culminates in the famous battle of Mahabharat where ultimately 'goodness' triumphed over 'evil'. These mythological characters along with a horde of realty—woman, down the ages, have nurtured, shaped the phyche and conscience of Indian society on concepts like women's rights, women emancipation and women empowerment. Women empowerment is not anathema to the virtues of Indian value system, although it is contemplated in the paradoxical plane of (a) 'meek surrender' at one end and (b) 'enlightened emergence' of 'women's self' at the other. The simultaneous emergence of these two contradicting forces is the real nuance of woman empowerment in India. As such any study on this concept should be made in terms of culture-specific parameters, distinctively different from its western form and essence.

The growing social awareness across the globe has brought about two significant issues into fore i.e., (a) gender equality and (b) empowerment of women. Discrimination against women is an indelible mark in a gender-based social system. Gender bias is an offshoot of extending biological differences into the domain of social placement. But over the years progressive outlook and strides of industrialization have greatly reshaped the thinking pattern of people. Consequent upon this change, treatment of women at par with men in every respect has gained currency, which quietly gives way to 'Women Empowerment'.

Empowerment of women thus touches the multidimensional plane of (i) equality between sexes, (ii) enhancement of skills, (iii) nurturing self-confidence and above all (iv) a meaningful participation in the decision making process.

Before starting a discussion on these highly correlated constituents, empowerment of women in present day India contemplates a glance at the state of Indian women in different spheres of life. According to the Human Development Report-2001, India ranks 105 in Gender Related Development Index (GDI) and 95 in Gender Empowerment Measure (GEM). Women literates constitute 44.5 per cent of the total literates. The percentage of women in Government and Ministerial level is 10.1, while the female economic activity is 42 per cent of the total economic activity. Despite considerable progress in the field of health and nutrition, the maternity mortality rate is 410 per 100,000 births. Let us look further into the reproductive health in India (Source: National Family Health Survey):

1. About 78 per cent of the conceptions that take place annually are unplanned and 25 per cent are definitely unwanted.
2. About 11 million abortions take place every year of which 6.7 per cent are induced and 4 million spontaneous. All these result in 15,000 to 20,000 deaths annually; practically all preventable.
3. Over 100,000 women die every year in the course of their physiological and social duty of pregnancy and childbirth and many times more than this number have a narrow escape not without significant physical and psychological injuries;
4. One in every 13 children dies within the first year of life. Infant mortality is 52 per cent higher in rural areas. Between 1-5 years age groups, girl child experiences 43 per cent higher mortality rate;
5. Female sterilization is 27 per cent against just 3.4 per cent of males.

The above statistics reveal a discouraging picture of women in the fields of (a) literacy, (b) employment in the organised sector, (c) awareness about health and hygiene, and (d) scope for 'choice living'. The presentation gets too dismal with the inclusion of the alarming incidence of rape, domestic violence, and harassment at workplace and other such crimes against women. The scenario further worsens with the effective representation of women in state legislatures and other local bodies and the consequent move to stall the process of Women's Reservation Bill being passed in the parliament by subversive groups. It is simply reiterated from the above facts that present day India lacks the basic sociological infrastructure to sensitise the society about women empowerment. One can not repudiate the fact also that the 21st century shining India is still glued to the regressive customs of (i) child marriages, (ii) early motherhood, (iii) female illiteracy, (iv) endemic insurgence of female infanticide, (v) polygamy, (vi) mass marriages on auspicious days, (vii) gang rapes, (vii) kidnapping and taming minor girls for the flesh markets. However, the other side of shinning India proudly pastes the success stories of numerous women entrepreneurs, athletes, artists, academicians, administrators, film makers, scientists, human rights activists, environmentalists, writers and above all politicians with enviable achievements in their respective fields.

So, the study of women empowerment in contemporary India is at cross-roads. But, to be figure specific, the vast array of success stories constitute only a quintessential part of the vast meadow of women oppression and indignity meted out to them from all corners of the society. Now the intriguing question still left unanswered is how to address this sensitive issue of women empowerment against the backdrop of eternal dichotomy and realistic dualism, which is the very essence of Indian sociological system. The dualism is finely turned into our thought, perception, and traditions irrespective of caste, creed and culture. Can this problem be well prevented only through the political will and concern ? Or some other extrinsic reinforcement is required to boost the morale of the long suffering women folk so as to enable themselves to smoothly come out of the oversized cocoons of patriarchy Yes. Yes 'something extra' is really needed to make them socially, economically, politically and ethically viable. In the present context that 'extra logistics support' can only be provided through adornment of a meaningful 'education base' specifically designed to benefit women.

It has been rightly observed by thinkers that education is the best contraceptive against all odds of women's lives. Political will and concern resulting in numerous legislations can bring out, at best, a gala of extrinsic support to the women folk, but certainly not their long cherished wish of 'substance' which is their dire need at this hour of crisis. Nothing except an appropriately developed, designed and viable education system replacing the existing non-specific education base can bring about the desired result. Because present day Indian women stand on the threshold of a new era in their endeavour to become full citizens assured of human rights and dignity. Through our constitution guarantees them through its fundamental rights, the rights of equality before law and equality of opportunity for education and employment, it is hardly assumed by the large masses of illiterate, semi literate and non enlightened women folk living in subhuman conditions of poverty, oppression and ignorance in the vast stretches of rural, semi urban and even urban areas of the great Indian state.

The existing system of education substantially lacks the skill to enthrall them to choose their own way and look after their families in a batter way. Women are the agents of change and education is considered a key instrument for their change; which is also vital for the national development. It will not be out of place to quote Napoleon's remark". Give me an educated mother, I shall promise you the birth of a civilized nation". It is also true of the saying that 'if you educate a boy you educate an individual, but if you educate a girl, you educate a family, society and ultimately the nation.' Women literacy rate is positively correlated with life-expectancy whereas illiteracy with poverty, deprivation and all other aspects of underdevelopment. Thus education liberates women from ignorance and enhances their self-esteem. So, education is the icon of empowerment.

Many strides have been made; still there are miles to go in this regard. Some of the major impediments are identified as (i) irrelevance of existing curriculum, (ii) distance of schools from dwellings, (iii) discriminating attitudes of teachers and parents disregard towards women's education, (iv) parents' illiteracy, (v) domestic labour, (vi) care of younger siblings, (vii) social taboos on the onset of puberty. These factors do not enable the girl child to receive education even if it is made 'compulsory' for children up to 14 years of age. Another appalling fact about female education is that since more than 50 per cent women are employed as wage labours, they have no time even to take primary education through formal or non formal education system.

But some of these relevant issues, have been aptly covered comprehensively in the New Education Policy 1986, the Plan of Action 1992, Sarva Sikhsya Abhijan 2001 (education for all, Ministry of Human Resource Development, Govt. of India) and Gyan Darshan (India's first education TV channel, by IGNOU). These are some staple endeavours on women's education front.

New innovations however are inevitably accompanied by new threats and fresh challenges. In the present millennium strategies for women empowerment must coordinate appropriate legislation with women's growing awareness on (a) health, (b) self-esteem, (c) social evil, (d) social reorientation; and (e) social justice. In this integrated effort, not only the role of the government, but also the role of NGOs, voluntary agencies, National and State Women Commissions assume utmost significance. A semblance needs to be made among the ethics and objectives of all these institutions who fight and care for women's causes, otherwise this very notion of empowerment will result in more deprivation and exploitation of women at the hands of unscrupulous agents or touts. Somewhere it could even lead to the emergence of unruly, arrogant and discourteous women's groups devoid of any benevolent fragrance either for themselves or for the nation as a whole. So great care, concern, compassion and caution are needed to develop an auto-balanced stream of women friendly national curriculum on female education which will empower women economically, socially, psychologically and ethically to enthral an aura of confidence and satisfaction in the environment where they live and let others live ever after happily satisfactorily and conscientiously.

And for all these wishes come true, the constitution of India women preamble should read like the following:

- We, the women of India have solemnly resolved to unite our collective wisdom for the betterment of our community and ourselves.
- We hereby vow to strive towards bringing peace and togetherness in our families and neighbourhood and work towards communal harmony.
- To educate ourselves, our men and our children about the values of compassion, love, integrity, honesty, truthfulness, hard work, acceptance, forgiveness, sharing, respect for humanity and our environment.
- To raise a collective voice against those indulging in suppression, oppression, exploitation, victimisation and abuse of ourselves, our men and our children.

- To strive towards social, economic and political justice, liberty of thought, expression, belief, faith, worship and equality of status and of opportunity for ourselves, our men and our children.

REFERENCE

1. *The Constitution of India Women Preamble,* Times Foundation, India times.

7

Role of Women in Indian Politics

A Study

Dr. (Smt.) Usha Padhy*

God created man and woman as equal. Both enjoyed equal status in society. During the Vedic period woman enjoyed comparatively high status. In this respect, India surpassed her contemporary civilization. Indian woman was looked upon as 'Sahadharmini' and equal partner of man in all walks of life. There are evidences of women scholars like Gargi,Maiteri, Lopamudra, Sabitri, Gayatri, Sarswati etc. In our culture Goddesses Laxmi, Saraswati, Durga, Ganga, and Rati have been honoured as the symbol of wealth, learning, strength, sacredness and beauty respectively. Our heritage also identifies that " Mother and motherland are superior to heaven". Our two great mythological epics, i.e. "the Ramayan and the Mahabharat" are heroine oriented stories.

Women possessed the concept of moral courage upon spiritual determination. She is the mother of the race and laison within generations. She is not only the source of symbol and progress but she can mould the future of the nation also.

With the passage of time, the status of women in India has undergone many changes. The advent of Muslim Rule in India compelled the women to be confined with in the four walls of the

* **Lecturer in Political Science and Principal, Savitri Women's College, Bhanjanagar.**

house. Still, women have shown their qualities at different times. She has talent, ability and confidence to work in all spheres of life. So, she should help to build up a progressive and developed society. Today, she has shown her capability more than man out side the home.

During the reign of Muslim and Mughals, the stutus of women in India was changed. She was suppressed. Many blind beliefs and superstitious practices encroached the liberty of the women. Her education suffered and she had very little role to play in the outside world. She was supposed to be a wonder full instrument for enjoyment. The influence of Western Education, the idea of great reformers and the leaders like Raja Ram Mohan Ray, Swami Dayananda Saraswati, Swami Vibekananda, Iswar Chandra Vidyasagar, Lokmanya Tilak, Mahatma Gandhi, Babasaheb Amabedkar, Sri Aurobinda and many others heralded a change in the status of woman. Lord William Bentinck, the then Governor General of India, abolished the system of sati in 1892 due to Raja Ram Mohan Roy who helped him in this task by giving many evidences from the sastras. Sri Roy and Swami Dayananda Championed the cause of woman like advocating the abolition of puradah system, child-Marriage system and introducing woman education and widow-marriage etc. They all advocated to give liberty to woman. Gandhi called woman to participate in the freedom movement. He told,"We can't achieve independence without woman who is half of the society".

The skill and ability of Tribhuban Mahadevi, Dandi Mahadevi, Ahalyabai, Sultana Rejiya, Jijabai and Padmini in war and administration became the landmark events all time to come.

During the first war of independence which was launched in 1857, Rani Laxmi Bai of Jhansi played an important role. Gradually, woman participated in large number in our Freedom movement.

Kamala Devi, Chattopadhyaya, Sarala Devi Choudhury, Sarala Roy, Abala Ghosh of Bengal, Vidya Gouri Nilakantha, Saradaben Meheta, Begum Hamid Alli of Gujarat; Sarala Devi, Rama Devi, Malati Devi etc. of Orissa had participation in the Freedom Movement. Srimati Bhikji Kama successfully created public opinion abroad towards the Freedom Movement. Sarojini Naidu was the first woman who actively participated in politics. Annie Beasant was the first lady president of Indian National Congress in 1917, Sarojini Naidu in 1925 and Smt. Indira Gandhi in 1959-60. On the call of Gandhiji, women rushed into the Freedom Movement. Queen Gaidin Lyoo of Nagalanda joined the movement in 1932 at the age of 13 and imprisoned till independence. Voluntary associations of women were formed by the leadership of Annie Beasant and her co-workers, i.e. Smt. Margarate Kausin, Queen Laxmibai Rajwada, Rajkumari Amrit Kaur, Rustamji Farriduji etc. Smt. Kasturaba Gandhi was behind the success of women participation in the Freedom Movement. Nehru told on the constructive role played by women that the future of India will probably depend ultimately more upon women than men.

The post-war reconstruction was not only meant for adjustments with each other in international life, but reconstruction of our national life also. There was a great demand from time to time with regard to the position of woman charter of rights and responsibilities.

There should be no dominance of one sex over the other nor exploitation of one by the other. The constitution, of the country guarantees equality between the sexes.

In 1929, for the first time, British Government accorded women the right to contest in Election. In the same year two women candidates contested from Madras Assembly. Between 1920 to 1942 women from different parts joined the Freedom Movement and showed their courage. Gandhi and Nehru both experienced the sincerity and ability of Indian women from Sarojini Naidu, Bijoy Laxmi Pandit, Amrit Kaur, Indira Gandhi etc., the then lady politicians. Women who can shoulder the responsibility in the society should be encouraged for higher education first and then to participate in politics. She should independently join politics, so that she can have a voice in Nation building and can help the cause of woman in general. A country like India, which was ruled by a powerful lady Prime-Minister i.e. Smt. Indira Gandhi and who was also a world statesman and had an effective voice in all policy making decision should boast amongst several women in the political field. During her period the glory of India was highlighted in home and abroad.

Today, woman participates from the kitchen house to Delhi Darwar. She has shown her ability in each faculty of our nation as Politician, Scientist, Engineer, Doctor, Pilot, Player, Administrator, Soldier etc. There were qualified lady politicians like Smt. Nandini Satapathy, Sucheta Kriplani, Susama Swaraj etc. who shouldered the responsibility as successful Chief Ministers of Orissa, Uttar Pradesh and Delhi. On the other hand the women politicians like Smt. Sonia Gandhi, Sushri Jayalalita and Mayabati who created crises in India and brought defame to this country in the world during the last part of 20th century.

The 73rd and 74th Amendment Acts reserved 33 per cent seats for woman in Rural and Local Urban bodies as councillors and chairpersons also. They appear by dint of quota system in the political arena through their male persons which we may call as 'Proxy Woman Participation'. In Bihar, proxy participation of Smt. Rabid Devi as Chief Minister was regulated by Lapu Prasad Yadav her husband and Ex-Chief Minister also.

No doubt, reservation for women is a way of inspiration specially to the rural women. It should not be taken as a political gain but for political upliftment of women in general.

It is observed that thirteen elections have been held to parliament in India from 1952 to 2004. In 1952, 14 women Parliamentarians were in Lok Sabha and 42 in 1989 which was the highest. Till now 10 per cent of women have not been elected to Loc Sabha nor the political parties select sufficient women candidates to contest in the elections. But the proposal raised top pass an Act for 33 per cent reservation of seats for women in the parliament and the State Assemblies which is seen as ridiculous. It is not for political progress of women but to create women Vote Bank like S.T., S.C., O.B.C. etc. The vested interest of the politicians should be checked utmost.

The positions of women is inferior to man in social set up is not only in developing countries like India, but in developed countries as well. The status of women throughout the world has been under going a lot of changes right from the ancient times. Advancement among women has become a global trend and symbol of modernizations.

On 8th March of 1970, the Russian Revolution was launched with 90,000 men and women. According to Trusky, "the Czar Administration would not be ended unless that was organized women participation." Since then the trend has been changed and women has been fighting for liberation and freedom in society. She demanded social, political and economic equality with man. Right to vote and right to contest was given in 1921 and 1929 respectively. After 2nd world war the United Nations was established on 24th October 1945. A commission was setup in 1946 by United Nations on the status of women and to accord political rights. In 1950 the General Assembly adopted the report of the commission and by 1971 all member countries of UN accepted and allowed political rights to women.

The people of a country like England elected Mrs. Margarte Thacher from conservative party as Prime Minister for three times. The active participation of women in politics as head of the government has been marked in South Asian countries. Sirimavo Bandarnik became the first lady Prime Minister of Srilanka and the world as well. Smt. Indira Gandhi drew the attention of the entire globe not only as the Indian Prime Minister but as a brilliant diplomat and statesman also. Benjir Bhatto of Pakisthan, Seikh Hassina Begum of Bangladesh, Chadrika Kumartunge of Srilanka have proved the ability of women as successful administrators.

The first international women congress was held at Maxico in 1975, at Copenhagen in 1980, at Nairobi in 1985 and in Beejing in 1995. 1985 was observed as International Women's year. All the above congress resolved to provide adequate facilities for equal participation of women with men.

In 1995 International Monetary Fund categorically specified in its report that unless women are given equal chance to formulate policies and to take political decisions in the state, a society can not progress.

It was reported by Inter Parliamentary Union that in 1988, women parliamentarians were 40.6 per cent in the world. But it was reduced to 11.7 per cent in 1997. In Britain it is 3-4 per cent in USA 2 per cent and in Germany 7-9 per cent. Now-a-days a trend has emerged to reserve seats in parliament for women especially in developing countries.

Our constitution guaranteed equality to all irrespective of gender in chapter III. It is gratifying to note that the Preamble of the charter of UN which, include India, accepts the position of equality between men and women. Long back of this charter, Indian National Congress passed a resolution on the fundamental rights in 1931. It runs as:- "All citizens are equal before the law irrespective of religion, caste, creed or sex. No disability attaches to any citizen by reason of his or her religion, caste, creed or sex in regard to public employment, office or power or honour to and in the increase of trade or calling."

The National Planning Committee formed under the National Congress, also passed a resolution in their meeting held on 30th August' 1940 that:

(a) In a planned society, women's place shall be equal to that of men. Equal status, equal opportunities and equal responsibilities shall be the guiding principles to regulate the status of women whatever the basis of society in the plan.

(b) Women shall not be excluded from any sphere of work merely on the ground of her sex.

(c) Marriage shall not be a condition precedent to the enjoyment of full and equal civic status and economic rights by women.

Several acts has been passed by Government to safeguard women. These include the Dowry Prohibition Act, 1961, the Indecent Representation of Women (Prohibition) Act, 1956, the Commission of Sati (Prohibition) Act, 1987, the Suppression of Immoral Traffic Act SITA 1956, etc.

In 1954, Taxation Enquire Committee was formed which advised the Government to take required step for social and economic development of women. In 1958, the Balwant Rai Mehta Committee reported about the weaker position of women in society. Still, no such remarkable step has been taken till 1980, through the Committee on the status of Indian women.

After Sahabanu case an Onus of Proof Act was passed which was for judicial protection to women in case of torture, oppression or injustice in society. The Department of Women and Child

Development has drawn up a National Prospective Plan for Women (1988-2000 AD) during Rajiv Gandhi regime. The Prime Minister P.V. Narasimha Rao also announced the setting of two commissions upon women upliftment. Also "Women's Studies" as a discipline is being encouraged in many universities as well as by the UGC. Seveal pro-women laws have been passed and women commissions at National and State level have been set up to protect their rights in different fields. However, these do not seem to be enough without social consciousness. Another feature for women development in Education. Without education it is not possible for anyone to understand his/her responsibility. So, emphasis should be given for women education.

'Women who constitute one half of the population are to participate in formulating plans, policies, programmes and projects of the nation. Keeping in view the burning necessity reservation of seats for women in Parliament and State assemblies, it is inevitable in the present contest. This matter was raised during the period at Sri H.D. Devgouda and Sri I.K. Gujral who brought it as 81st Constitutional Amendment Bill, 1988. It was strongly opposed by Mulayam Singh Yadev, Sarad Yadav, Kumari Mayabati in a plea for reservation of SC, ST, OBC, Women. Again it has been put into the dead box. Bajpayee Govt. revived this Bill, but failed.

It is seen that South Africa, Uganda, Mojambik and Sweeden have reserved seats for women in polities which has created consciousness about women development. Many more social problems of women have been taken up in these countries. A country like India where women is worshipped as mother Goddess till no such initiatives has been taken for such an act. It may be suggested that the Reservation Act for women should be passed which should include two clouses; first woman should be taken as a class but not be divided into other categories which is meant nasty politics. This decision was given by our supreme court in 1992 also. Secondly, no woman should be represented from such a family, who already represents in parliament earlier.

Recently, the Supreme Court has given a historic decision about the identification of children by mother as coequal to father. It enhanced the position of women in our state. Besides, all the papers/

certificates of all examinations are seem to be incorporated the mother's name of each and every student/pupil. It is a matter of praiseworthy for the motherland.

Men and women constitute the society. They are just two sides of a coin. Women are one half of the humanity. But naturally all are unequal. Each and everyone differs to each other and complementary to each other. So also woman differs from man in her physical features, feelings, sphere of work, temperament and qualities. Women have created the race, enlightened the nation and Sacrificed for the state. Mahatma Gandhi aptly told, "I am firmly of opinion that Indians salvation depends on the sacrifice and enlightenment of their women."

There is no ultimatum to mother, the creator. She is the apex of a state. We call our country as Bharatmata. Manu, the first law giver of the world wrote in Chapter II (145) of Manu Smriti,'Acharya is tentimes superior to Upadhyaya, father is hundred times superior to Acharya and mother is thousand times superior to father.' She is the maker of the nation.

Women today are storming all the male bastions and proving themselves to be equally good in all most all walks of life. Women in India today are also poised to take off. They are standing on the threshold of a new era. It should be realized that "every issue is a woman's issue" from water to militarization, violence to economic planning, ecology to economic development and from kitchen to parliament.

There can be no two opinions that women today can no longer be regarded as weaker sex and discriminates against as second class citizen. They have self-confidence on their capability. They are talent, calibre, efficient, sincere, hardworking, straight forward, practical and principled to march ahead. Reservation hints their self-conceit and sentiment. She should not be an issue in politics. So, 60.8 per cent of women oppose the Reservation.

Women are making efforts round the world to see that their rights are respected, their voices heeded, their opportunities widened. The "voice from the kitchen' is being heard in International Forum. They should be brought into the mainstream of national development not as beneficiaries but as contributors and partakers along with men, and as rightful claimants of Social Security. Let us all strive to give women the place they so richly and rightfully deserve in society. The hand that rocks the cradle rules the world.

The women always think that they should be ideal for the society. They should not defame the position of the nation in general and status of women in particular by playing nasty politics. Otherwise the nation may loose its identity for ever. So, women should be at par with men in every walk of life in all spheres.

REFERENCES

1. Satish Chandra, *Medieval India*, Part-I, New Delhi, 1978.
2. Dr. B.C. Ray, *Orissa Under the Mughals*, Calcutta, 1981.
3. T.P. Saxena, *Women in Indian History*, New Delhi, 1979.
4. S. Ram Sharma (ed) *Women and Education*, New Delhi,1979.
5. Anjana Maitra-Sinha, *Women in a Changing Society*, New-Delhi, 1993.
6. Dr. B.K. Sharma, Wadhintra Angramare Utkaliya Nari, Berhampur, 1990.
7. The Sambad, 20.7.92, 16.2.97, 09.3.97, 8.6.97.
8. The Samaj, 1.11.87, 7.2.88, 27.3.88, 12.6.88, 16.7.89, 23.9.90, 12.4.92, 9.5.93, 8.3.98, 28.2.99.
9. The Prajatantra, 14.5.89, 1.2.94, 7.5.94, 30.11.95, 19.12.96, 27.3.98, 18.8.98, 8.3.99.
10. Birendra Kumar Panda (ed.), *Veda Piyusha*, Vol/X, No. 8, January 1999 Bhadrak.

8

Women Lagging Behind in the Era of Women Empowerment

A Study on Ganjam District

Santosh Kumar Pradhan

Introduction

Gender discrimination became an alarming danger which creates several types of violation due to inequalities and disparities. This create the need of women to facilitate more by legal safeguard with different policy measures. After several measures on women empowerment and steps to reduce gender disparity, Ganjam district have such lacunas which needs more careful steps to be taken for fulfilment of women empowerment measures.

Wages of Agricultural Labours

Major of the working force depend on agriculture, but the job opportunities is not all time in this sector, so the demand for labour forced is raised only the time of harvesting and cropping season, in this manner the wages rate is not satisfactory as compare to the other sector. The average daily wages of different classes of agricultural labourers in study district narrated in the following Table—8.1.

Table—8.1: Average daily wages of different classes of agriculture labourers in Ganjam District

Type of agriculture labour		*Average daily wages per manday (in Rs)*	
		1997-98	*1998-99*
(A)	**Agricultural Field labours**		
1.	Men	32.27	37.55
2.	Women	24.95	29.05
3.	Children	18.32	27.96
(B)	**Other Agricultural labours**		
1.	Men	36.16	40.75
2.	Women	25.89	28.49
3.	Children	20.00	25.26

Source: District Statistical Hand Book, Ganjam, 1999, p. 102.

The above Table—8.1 reveals that the average daily wages of agricultural labour is not satisfactory as their devote hard work as compare with other sector labourers. The average daily wages also raised up in the year 1998-99. But it is not so sufficient where as compression between the agriculture field labour with other agriculture labour, the daily wages paid to man, women and children was high rate in case of other agriculture labour in 1997-98. But in 1998-99 only man of other agriculture labour gets higher wage as compare to the agriculture field labour. Women and children of agriculture labour gets more wages as compare with the women and children of other agriculture labours.

Employment

Employment generates the living standard of the people. Unemployment causes poverty and it will create certain hurdles to achieve the basic objectives of the planning process of the district as well as State.

Unemployment will be acute in the rural areas of the district. Unless a proper care is taken by the Government, Semi-Government, Public Sector Undertakings and non-Government Organisations, will cause acute problems, for the growth and development of the district. The Table—8.2 highlights the unemployment as per qualification wise, along with live registers of the district during the year 1994.

The Table—8.2 reveals that the registered in metric level i.e. highest. The placement of persons will regard to the register unemployment is very negligible.

Table—8.2: Employment registration record of Ganjam district as on 31st December'1999

Sl. No.	Category	Below Metric	Metric	Under Graduate	General Technical	General Graduates	Diploma Holders	PG
1.	Total Registration out of which	1,824	6,556	2,737	959	2,222	206	200
	(a) Women	39	771	529	380	521	09	81
	(b) SC	168	937	330	47	161	08	06
	(c) ST	83	109	18	13	07	01	01
2.	Total Placement out of which	93	177	19	39	34	10	12
	(a) Women	–	31	07	09	16	–	03
	(b) SC	17	32	08	01	03	–	–
	(c) ST	14	45	05	04	03	–	–
3.	Total live Register Position at the end of the year Out of which	9,822	30,432	8,503	3,598	8,019	1,138	729
	(a) Women	1,044	2,776	1,497	1,236	1,476	29	250
	(b) SC	3,067	4,662	872	170	500	56	31
	(c) ST	454	334	42	38	38	07	04

Source: Statistical Hand Book Ganjam, 1999, p. 100.

Wage Structure

Wage is the prime indicates of the labourers for changing their living style of all the problems, that face the labourer, that of wages is the most pressing and persistent. Wage is lone of the important incentive which influences the labour supply in numerous productive activities. Since, wage is the only source of income (in from of cash/kind) substantial amenities like purchasing of food, health care, education, and other social risk are fulfilled. In case of agricultural labourer their average income is derived from wage and employment. Thus, the living condition of agricultural labourers depends on wage rate. Wages of agricultural labourers depends on condition like climate, output, rainfall, demand and supply during the time of harvesting, to plant seedling and showing period. During the employment period it is difficult task for fixing the hour of normal working day in agriculture operation with measuring the value of wage rate that are paid by kind. They are always received lower real wage because of non-existence of labour market, non-adequate labour organisation among them self in agrarian sector. The agricultural labourers always acquainted with misery.

The average daily wages of different classes of agricultural labourer in Ganjam district clearly mentioned in Table—8.3.

Table—8.3: Average daily wage of different classes of agricultural labourer in Ganjam District (1998-99)

	Types of rural labourer	*Average daily wages per man-day (Rs.)*
A.	**Skilled labourer:**	
(i)	Carpenter	77.19
(ii)	Mason	81.35
(iii)	Tractor Driver	84.90
B.	**Agricultural field labourers:**	
(i)	Men	37.55
(ii)	Women	29.05
(iii)	Children	27.96
C.	**Other Agricultural labourers:**	
(i)	Men	40.75
(ii)	Women	28.49
(iii)	Children	25.26

Source: District Statistical Handbook, Ganjam, 1999, p. 102.

The above table reveals that the average daily wages per man-day in 1998-1999 shown that the wage rate of skilled labourer are 77.19 Rupees for Carpenter, 81.35 Rupees for mason and 84.90 Rupees for Tractor driver, whereas in case of agricultural field labourer men gets Rs. 37.55, women Rs. 29.05, and children Rs.

27.96 respectively and other agricultural labourer men gets Rs. 40.75, women Rs. 28.39 and children Rs. 25.26 but in actual they did not received same amount fixed by the Government. Even after the launching of different five-year plans the socio economic status of agricultural persistency classes is far from physiological expectations. It is lamentable to note that the wage structure in agrarian society is fully rigidity rather then flexibilities this is because of the following reasons:

(i) Like the industrial sector there is no strong trade union, association to protect against the vast interest of the agricultural labourers.

(ii) A large segment of agricultural labourers are seasonal employed in a year. They don't get full timework rather they work only stipulated time period.

(iii) Majorities of agricultural labourers are unskilled they don't possess adequate training facilities, specifies educational qualification and knowledge on modern technology.

(iv) Most of the agricultural labourers are poverty ridden this compels them to work subsistence wage rates.

(v) Since the agriculture sector does not provides alternative job avenues. Then the agricultural labourers are highly consented on agricultural sector.

To give a moral boost and economic justice the Government has adopted the Minimum Wage Act policy in 1948. The basic objectives of the Minimum Wage Act are not only to support of the subsistence wage, but also it is imperative to provide education, medical requirement and amenities. But this policy is totally inapplicable in case of agricultural labourers because they totally unknown about the method to protect for fulfil their demand by the strong union.

Education

Education enriches and expands the mental and physical Horizon of people but unfortunately the impact of education has not been percolated to the agricultural families. Hence, majority of the agricultural families are illiterate.

Unaccounted of their literacy they deny their children to attend the school, because they will employ them in their farm thus they deprived from the primary education, the dropout rate of school children is very high on account of following reasons.

(i) Illiterate and ignorant parents.

(ii) Poverty/economic problems.

(iii) Non-stimulating social environment.

(iv) Early marriage.

(v) Discouraging School environment.

The dropout rate from primary, middle and secondary school state wise is given in Table—8.4. The Table—8.4 reveals that the total droptout rates of different states with union territories indicates that the dropout rates from class VIII-X is high then the class I-V and class VI-VII Gross dropout rates of state skim is high where as in Keral is lowest. In case of Orissa the total dropout rates in case up girls is higher then the rates of boys at all stages of schooling. The total from classes VIII-X were 72.52 , and the dropout rates for boys were 72.93 per cent and girls were 71.90 per cent.

Low level of literacy makes them educational backward, consequently they don't par with other labourers due to lack of education the various programmes, policies lunched by the Government and other agency hamper for implementation in proper manner. They are ignorant about modern technology, high yield seeds, using pesticides, multi-cropping, export qualities of food-grains, self-employment etc. Due to this they are unaware about the health hazardous, malnutrition, environmental degradation, with standard of living, they purely unknown about the marketing system for selling their product in correct rate, they always smuggling and cheating by the trading person.

Fooding

Good calories food always helps for mankind lives standardization with comfortable life. Adequate nutrition is also essential to have a healthy productive working population. Adequate nutrition of children and adults is increasingly being seen as basic human rights. Although the agricultural labourers

Table—8.4: Gross Dropout Rates (in percentage) in classes' I-V, VI-VII and VIII-X, 1999-2000 (provisional)

States	*(Class I-V)*			*(Class VI-VII)*			*(Class VIII-X)*		
	Boys	*Girls*	*Total*	*Boys*	*Girls*	*Total*	*Boys*	*Girls*	*Total*
1	*2*	*3*	*4*	*5*	*6*	*7*	*8*	*9*	*10*
Andhra Pradesh	39.42	41.23	40.28	64.32	69.06	66.52	76.53	77.67	77.02
Arunachal Pradesh	49.77	50.81	50.23	66.07	63.38	64.92	74.93	77.64	76.08
Assam	25.85	42.20	33.69	68.05	71.99	69.81	81.32	77.92	76.80
Bihar	56.50	58.64	57.27	75.75	80.96	77.62	-35.19	87.42	83.46
Delhi	5.36	6.03	5.67	21.37	9.03	15.23	43.20	-56.03	-45.46
Goa	5.83	11.51	5.58	7.14	13.27	10.12	70.60	42.42	42.83
Gujarat	30.51	28.10	29.49	57.46	65.37	60.99	42.75	74.87	72.52
Haryana	16.09	12.78	14.57	26.35	36.38	31.04	38.36	52.54	47.16
Himachal Pradesh	36.63	33.90	35.35	25.48	27.29	26.35	61.89	42.57	40.37
Jamu and Kashmir	55.12	47.39	51.84	32.48	44.99	37.61	68.53	71.22	65.80
Karnataka	30.32	27.19	28.87	59.82	65.35	62.47	29.10	69.36	68.92
Keral	–9.03	–5.00	–7.05	–7.33	–4.06	–5.73	62.21	18.17	23.74
Madhya Pradesh	16.02	22.97	19.03	41.01	55.23	47.15	53.72	76.41	68.38
Maharashtra	18.99	21.72	20.29	17.51	42.95	29.59	76.56	60.92	57.10
Manipur	43.66	42.90	43.30	42.92	43.25	43.08	61.26	75.48	76.06
Meghalaya	57.63	57.22	57.43	77.82	77.66	77.74	76.10	63.09	62.13

(Table Contd...)

1	2	3	4	5	6	7	8	9	10
Mizoram	51.96	51.27	51.64	68.01	63.36	65.81	71.62	73.19	74.72
Nagaland	46.78	46.68	46.73	43.55	36.47	40.27	72.93	69.87	70.83
Orissa	27.87	44.38	36.12	63.32	62.05	62.81	35.37	71.90	72.52
Punjab	24.57	20.15	22.49	29.82	29.90	29.86	79.27	35.73	35.54
Rajasthan	46.00	62.68	52.53	38.76	56.09	44.89	88.57	83.73	80.74
Sikkim	61.27	56.35	58.94	73.11	67.12	70.33	59.75	87.47	88.06
Tamil Nadu	42.70	39.19	41.10	44.63	41.61	43.22	78.06	57.63	58.77
Tripura	49.66	49.25	49.47	67.94	68.58	68.24	55.48	79.30	78.63
Uttar Pradesh	53.11	62.16	56.64	50.37	57.94	53.01	79.01	72.92	61.56
West Bengal	49.85	58.48	54.07	70.04	71.99	70.88	83.09	85.45	82.06
Union Territories									
Andaman & Nicobar Island	5.52	5.77	5.64	32.54	34.25	33.37	45.53	44.21	44.90
Chandigarh	67.15	66.17	−66.70	−3.06	−4.76	−3.88	18.24	5.96	12.60
Dadra & Nagar Haveli	23.69	41.29	31.53	53.85	61.53	57.04	75.22	79.21	76.97
Daman & Diu	0.76	6.60	3.59	2.06	4.13	3.06	42.29	46.66	44.30
Lakshdweep	1.58	4.08	2.70	24.79	25.06	24.92	45.42	43.77	44.65
Pondicherry	−6.44	−6.19	−6.32	0.85	−0.33	0.29	43.27	38.99	4.23
India	38.67	42.28	40.25	51.96	58.00	54.53	66.58	70.60	68.28

Source: India, Ministry of Human Resources Development, Department of Elementary and Literacy (2001). Annual Report 2000-01, New Delhi, p. 223-225.

Dropout rates relate to the year 1997-98.

Table—8.5: Consumption capacity of agricultural families in per meals (in Grams)

Items	*Good calories of foods*		*Foods or agricultural families*					
			Children (Categories)			*Adults (Categories)*		
	Children	*Adults*	*Middle*	*Low*	*Worse*	*Middle*	*Low*	*Worse*
Rice	150 Gms	250 Gms	100 Gms	80 Gms	60 Gms	200 Gms	150 Gms	100 Gms
Wheat	150 Gms	250 Gms	–	–	–	–	–	–
Dal	50 Gms	100 Gms	–	–	–	–	–	–
Sugar	50 Gms	100 Gms	–	–	–	–	–	–
Fresh Fruits	50 Gms	150 Gms	–	–	–	–	–	–
Fresh Vegetable	100 Gms	150 Gms	–	–	–	–	–	–
Other Vegetable	75 Gms	150 Gms	50 Gms	15 Gms	5 Gms	75 Gms	50 Gms	30 Gms
Edible Oil	35 Gms	100 Gms	5 Gms	2 Gms	–	15 Gms	10 Gms	–
Fish/Meat	30 Gms	150 Gms	–	–	–	–	–	–
Egg	1 Pic	2 pic	–	–	–	–	–	–

Source: Compiled from questionnaire.

contributing thousands tonnes of food production for feeding the millions mouth at the same time they have nothing available for their self-substance, out of their own production they use the some items for their self-consumption. The following Table—8.5 reflected about the comparison based on necessary of good calories food for a person with consumption capacities of agricultural labour per day meal.

The above table reveals that the family member of agrarian society always consumed less calories with a shortage quantity of food items, intake of food hamper. Their energy, efficiency and integrity. This hampers their vigorous health and doesn't promote robust body. This generates malnutrition problem. In case of consumption capacity of agrarian children found that good calories food is not applicable for them low and worse categories food always consumed. Adults group communities have no capacities to consume good calories of food, all of them consume low standard food in their per day meals.

Food and Nutrition is always helps for better standard of living for every human being but to find about the nutrition requirements of children up to 12 years is not so sufficient is a agrarian society. The intake of nutrition's by children in different age group is given the Table—8.5.

The following table revels that the energy requirements of children up to 12 years were not being adequately met. The requirement and Vitamin-A for all Ages was also inadequate both boys and girls.

Due to lack of balanced diet and consuming unhygienic food they suffer from food allergic, food poison with suffering diseases like cough, cholera, night blind, jaundice, fever, dysentery, diarrhoea, respiratory diseases etc. Sometimes they face death, these problems are not admitted them as their problems, and they are thinking blind believes as witchery because of unknown about the food scarcity problems.

Health

Agriculture is such culture there is no leisure and pleasure, in this manner agricultural labour endeavour their laborious power

Table—8.6: Average intake of nutrients according to age and sex

Age Group	*Sex*	*Protein*	*Fats*	*Energy*	*Calcium*	*IRON*	*Thiamin*	*Ribof lavin*	*Niacin*	*Vit-C*	*Vit-A*
		(Gms)	*(Gms)*	*(K cal)*	*(Mg)*	*(Mg)*	*(Mg)*	*(Mg)*	*(Mg)*	*(Mg)*	*(Mg)*
1-3	Boys	30.1	16.3	918.1	414.5	8.9	0.69	0.50	7.4	28.5	195.5
	Girls	30.5	15.6	925.9	395.0	9.2	0.70	0.50	7.9	30.1	200.8
4-6	Boys	40.6	20.3	1299.5	432.9	13.0	1.03	0.62	11.1	37.4	249.8
	Girls	41.2	19.1	1298.5	439.6	11.3	1.03	0.63	11.3	38.9	240.7
7-9	Boys	50.0	21.6	1570.3	468.2	20.0	1.37	0.72	13.5	41.5	258.4
	Girls	49.7	23.5	1520.0	472.1	18.3	1.12	0.80	15.8	43.3	246.5
10-12	Boys	56.8	24.9	1847.0	521.9	18.7	1.52	0.83	16.2	50.0	306.6
	Girls	45.7	20.3	1482.2	425.9	15.1	1.23	0.68	13.0	39.6	309.8
13-15	Boys	67.1	28.8	2184.9	612.4	22.1	1.82	1.00	19.6	57.4	356.3
	Girls	65.6	28.4	2097.1	615.4	21.4	1.71	0.98	18.7	60.1	369.4

Source: India, Ministry of Human Resources Development, Dept. of Women and Chid Development Food and Nutrition Board, India Nutrition Profile, p. 14, 15, 1998.

for feeding to million starvation and hungry people, but to find about the health condition of family of agricultural labourer are very worse then the other sector labourer. In every organised sector there must be settle medi-care unity for their labourer, their own dispensary with the medical staff ready for given treatment facilities into their labourer as well as their family members. But in case of agrarian sector there is no separate unit of dispensary actives for health care facilities to them, primary level treatment is better for them with the natural medi-care items. In the organised sector all types of health care facilities are given by the authorities to their labourer like medical advanced, medical allowance, sick leave facilities etc. But in case of agricultural labourer these facilities are dream for them. In this manner it is clearly remarks that the health condition of agrarian society; is very bad.

Health is a matter of basic self-care with the psychological, mental as well as physical rest is necessary, ill health no longer seen as an unexplained evil, which needs professional magical remedies to cure. But agrarian families self care are always unrest physical as well as mental rest is not applicable for them. So the families are survivable with suffering great diseases with; incurable method, they die with easily preventable disease. In the general health status like crude death rate, infant mortality, life expectancy, prevention and control of communicable diseases, environmental sanitation, maternal and childcare are the hidden way indicators in the agrarian society.

Besides this a series of orthodoxies dogmatic fanaticism method such as enchanting mantras, offering animal, birds to the Goddesses to avoid the severe diseases like cholera, typhoid, mnemonic, chicken plus, pox and other diseases, can be offered as a supreme example.

To find out the good health condition of the population in a society, the major indications are reflecting to study about the matter like Infant Mortality Rate (IMR), Maternal Mortality Rates (MMR), Expectation of life etc. where as infant mortality rates can also contribute to the cause of the development of a nation. The Infant Mortality Rate in the states and union territories along with major causes of child death also explained on the Tables—8.7 and 8.8.

Table—8.7: Child labourer at different age group and sex

Different age	Male child labour	Female child labour	Total
0-5	11	26	37
5-10	116	117	233
10-15	172	58	230
Total	**299**	**201**	**500**

Source: Compiled from questionnaire.

The Table—8.7 reveals that the highest IMR is in rural areas of the state Orissa was 99 and 66 in urban area where as in based of all India it was 74 in rural and 43 in case of urban area. This high level IMR in rural area indicates the health condition of agrarian society, high female illiteracy, along with the problems of lack of access to health services in remote rural, hilly, tribal areas are the major factors associated with high IMR.

The major causes of informant child death are premature birth, acute respiratory infection, diarrhoeal diseases; vaccine preventable diseases were immunisation coverage has not reached optimal levels, and inadequate material and new born care. The major causes of infant death by major age groups are as given Table—8.8.

Table—8.8: Estimated Infant Mortality Rate (IMR) by Rural-Urban States, 2000

Name of State	Total	Rural	Urban
1	2	3	4
Andhra Pradesh	65	74	36
Assam	75	78	35
Bihar	62	63	53
Gujarat	62	69	45
Haryana	67	69	57
Karnatak	57	68	24
Kerala	14	14	14
Madhya Pradesh	88	94	54
Maharashtra	48	57	33

(Table Contd...)

1	2	3	4
Orissa	96	99	66
Punjab	52	56	38
Rajasthan	79	83	58
Tamil Nadu	51	57	38
Uttar Pradesh	83	87	65
West Bengal	51	54	37
Arunachal Pradesh	44	45	11
Chhatisgarh	79	95	49
Delhi	32	32	32
Goa	23	24	21
Jharkhand	70	74	48
Himachal Pradesh	60	62	37
Jammu & Kashmir	50	51	45
Manipur	23	23	25
Meghalaya	58	61	32
Mizoram	21	24	15
Nagaland	NA	NA	23
Sikkim	49	49	36
Tripura	41	42	32
Uttaranchal	50	73	26
Union Territories			
Andaman & Nicobar	23	27	10
Chandigarh	28	38	26
Dadra & Nagar Haveil	58	62	14
Daman & Diu	48	38	57
Lakshadweep	27	25	29
Pondicherry	23	33	15
India*	68	74	43

Source: India Registrar General, Vital Statistics Division, (2001). Sample Registration System Bulletin, October 2001, New Delhi, p. 1.

Note: 1. NA- Not available due to part-receipt of returns.

2. Infant Mortality rate for Smaller States and Union Territories for 1998-2000.

* Excludes Nagaland (Rural) due to part-receipt of returns.

The Table—8.8 reveals that the causes of prematurely is high per cent than the other cases in the case of all states. In case of Orissa the percentage of prematurely was 38.5 in the year 1997 and diarrhoea of new born was 0.5 lower levels.

Child Labour at different Age Groups and Sex

A baby below the age of 15 years is cered as child. The children are classified into three age groups, one 0-5 years two, 5- 10 years, and third is 10-15 years. The sample Child Labourer of the district Ganjam is illustrated in the Table—8.7 and graph 8.1.

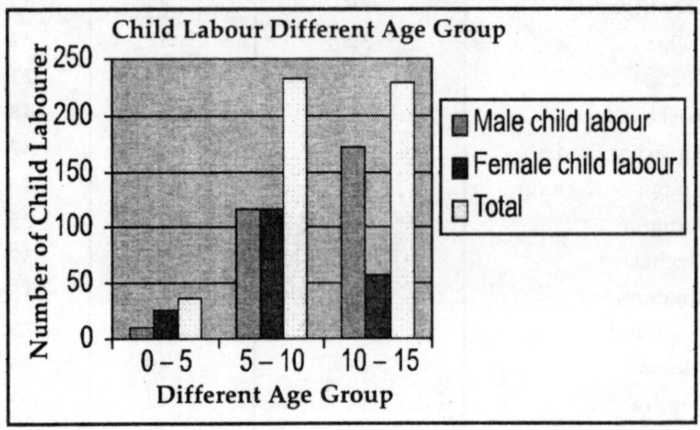

From the Table—8.7 it reveals that out of 500 samples, 299 numbers of male child labourers are covered with 60 per cent engaged in agricultural sector. But it is 201 numbers of female child labourers as covered with 40 per cent engaged in agriculture sector.

The female child labourer in the age group of 0-5 and 5-10 years is bit higher than the male child labourer, but they reduced with the age group of 10-15 years. This may be caused due to, with the grown up age the family members do not allow their female child to work in the agriculture fielded. This is also explained in the graph 8.2.

Child Labour According to Caste

The sample labourer of the district Ganjam are divided into different caste like—General, Scheduled Caste and Scheduled Tribe. Out of 500 samples taken for the study purpose are divided as per the caste is illustrated in the Table—8.9 and also in graph 8.2.

Table—8.9: Caste wise child labourer working in the agricultural sector

Caste	*Male child labour*	*Female child labour*	*Total*
General	83	34	117
SC	100	68	168
ST	116	99	215
Total	**299**	**201**	**500**

Source: Compiled from questionnaires.

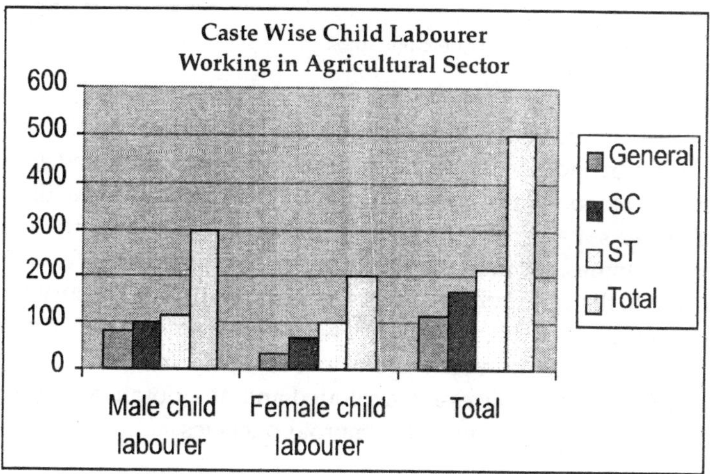

According to Table—8.9. The child labourers are highest in Schedule Tribe category as compared to Schedule Caste and General. It is lowest in General Caste.

According to Family Size

Generally in rural areas the children are working in the agricultural field due to big size family. Owing to big size family the father and mother are not able to take care of their children for providing food even once a day. So a child is compelled to working in the agriculture field. This is explained in the Table—8.10.

Table—8.10: Children are working in the agricultural field according to their family Size.

Family Size	*Male child labour*	*Female child labour*	*Total*
2-5	11	03	14
5-8	47	63	110
8-11	63	59	122
11-14	78	47	125
14 & above	100	29	129
Total	**299**	**201**	**500**

Source: Compiled from questionnaires.

Summary

From the above discrimination, it is revealed that the social economic conditions of agricultural labourer are pitiable and ensure mountable comparing to the other sector labourer. In Ganjam district of Orissa state agriculture is the prime stage for searching the job opportunities, but the agricultural sector can not be assets for sound health to the agrarian society, misery is the main path for survive to life. They spent their rest of life with bereavement, poverty and penuries. Their innocent agony is inevitable forever. They are suppressed and oppressed, exploited and deteriorated by the big land lords, middleman and numerous agencies.

Wage is the measuring path for standard of living of any sector labourer, but to known about the wage structure of agricultural labourer in the study district, they are always receiving low wage rates as comparing to other sector. This low wage rate fostering them to living in unhinge manner with consuming less calories food, wearing low standard cloth, away from education, uncomfortable shelter, unhealthy condition in all time believing their own luck.

Till end of he 21st century the plight condition of the agricultural labourer have not been mitigated. They are born in agriculture live in agriculture and die in agriculture with indebtedness, in this consequence they don't provide basics requirement of life to the members of such big families. In this situation, child labour is a must and most of the child labourers are in domestic work with agriculture field, which will be impediment for economic progress in agrarian society.

REFERENCES

1. Registrar General, Vital Statistics Division. (2001), Govt. of India. Sample Registration System Bulletin, October 2001, New Delhi, p. 1.

2. Ministry of Human Resources Development, Dept. of Women and Child Development Food and Nutrition Board, India Nutrition Profile, Govt. of India, p. 14, 15. 1998.

3. Ministry of Human Resources Development, Department of Elementary and Literacy, Govt. of India (2001). Annual Report 2000-01, New Delhi, p. 223-225.

4. District Statistical Handbook, Ganjam, 1999, 2000, 2001.

5. Orissa Reference Annual, 2001.

9

Some Legal Provisions in Respect of Women Empowerment

Sri Surendranath Panda

God has created this universe. He is the Almighty. We the ereatiures enjoy the benefit of the universe. But at times we see deviation from the normal way of life because of our activities. Human beings are the noble creatures of the God. For our survival God has created water, air, forest and all other natural properties. But don't follow the natural law. So in each and every field the ecological imbalance not only affects our natural growth but also hurts our mental fertility creating troubles in normal life. So to strengthen the activities and punish the culprits, laws are enacted by way of legislation for welfare of the society.

Men and women are the two sides of the same coin. If one side is damaged, then the same will be out of circulation. Men and women are inseparable in nature. Women nearly constitute 50 per cent of the total population of the world. But now-a-days the male female ratio is declining day by day because of our ignorance.

India has a glorious past. We depend on the tradition and culture of our country since time immemorial we are inclined to have a son. As per our belief we require a son or *'putra'* to save us from PUT (means Papa or Sorrow). Because of this belief, we need a sone in stead of a daughter. But now-a-day the scenario has already been changed. Girl child has achieved in almost all field in comparison to male child. But to provide social status, economical independence and political achievement almost all the countries have adopted new laws to bring a reform in the society particularly in cases of girl child and women. The following table gives us an alarming picture of regarding declining of female ratio in comparison to male.

Table—9.1:

Year	*Orissa*	*India*
1941	1053	945
1951	1022	946
1961	1001	941
1971	988	930
1981	981	934
1991	972	927
2001	–	933

Many legislations have already been enacted to safeguard the girl child. 1979 observed by the United Nations as the International year of the child. Similarly the SAARC countries declared 1990 as the Year of Girl Child in order to highlight their problems as well as to solve those problems by way of mutual co-operation.

The following table will also show the percentage of female literacy in our country. This table clearly indicates that the literacy rate in respect of women in not upto the mark.

Table—9.2: Female literacy in India

Year	*Literacy ratio in %*
1901	0.06
1911	1.05
1921	1.81
1931	2.93
1941	7.30
1951	7.39
1961	12.05
1971	16.69
1981	24.82
1991	39.42
2001	54.16

After considering the problems of girl child their percentage of literacy and their work pattern different legislations of India have been enacted to provide equality as well as equity to them. Our Constitution also provides facilities to them. There are some National Statutes to save them from exploitation. The notable Acts are Child Labour (Prohibition and Regulation) Act, Child Marriage Restraint Act, 1929, Guardianship and Wards Acts, Hindu Minority and Guardianship Act, 1956, India Majority Act 1875 and many others. The problems of women are also dealt by some provisions of following Acts:

- Code of Criminal Procedures, 1973;
- Immoral Traffic Prevention Act, 1965;
- Indian Contract Act, 1872;
- Indian Endence Act, 1872;
- Indian Panel Code, 1860;
- Probation of Offenders Act, 1958;
- Special Marriage Act, 1954.

Judicial and Quasi-Judicial institutions like family court, Women Commission, Women Welfare Board, Social Welfare Boards of Centre and States are also established to deal with the problems of the women.

The United Nations General Assembly has also proclaimed the year 1975 as the International Women's Year. Similarly, the United Nations declared 1975-1985 as the Decade for women.

The basic idea of UN Assembly was to promote intensified action in welfare of the women. Our Constitution guarantees Justice, Liberty and Equality to all its citizens. Similar, provisions are also prescribed specially for protection of women under Articles 15(3), 16, 39, 51 (A) (e).

Criminal activities against women are rising day by day. Such crimes can be categorised as dowry torture, domestic violence, rape adultery, marriage and divorce, maintenance etc. But, to check all these crimes many legislations has been created. Dowry Prohibition Act provides that both giving and taking dowry is an offence. Indian Penal Code was amended and a new Section 499 (A) was introduced in 1983 providing punishment and also fine to the husband and his relatives if they are involved in cruelty towards women. Section 494 of I.P.C. is also a commendable provision to check polygamy.

Hindu law was codified in the year 1955 and 1956 in the field of marriage, succession, adoption and maintenance etc. Section 5 of Hindu Marriage Act provides that a Hindu having living spouse cannot have a valid marriage with another. In 1978 Hindu Marriage Act was amended and the age of both bride and groom are prescribed which is a mile stone in the Hindu Marriage, Section 376 of IPC prescribes punishment to the rape culprit. The introduction of 114(A) in the Evidence Act is definitely a positive thought in the law of Evidence to deal rape case which is heinous in nature. Hindu Adoption and Maintenance Act of 1956 gives wide scope to women to adopt son and daughter and at the same time to claim maintenance. Section 18 of the same Act ensures the right of separate residence of the wife in addition to her maintenance. Section 125 of the CrPC also gives enough opportunity to the wife and girl child to claim maintenance against husband and parents respectively. Hindu succession Act of 1956 provides a property right to Hindu Women, abolishing the concept of limited estate.

Women's right participation in political arena is guaranteed by International Conventions. In our country participation of women in Panchayat Raj System and Nagara Palika System are introduced. Large number of women participate in the political arena. But they should also be given the same opportunity in Assembly and Parliament elections. In the year 1995 the 4th world conference on women was convened at Beijing in China and some basic principles were focused for alround development of the women and those were as follows:

- Violence (including domestic violence) against women must be dropped.
- Girls must be given importance against the boys in their family as well as in the society.
- Women must have access to quality education, health care, economic independence and political power.
- Family responsibility must be shared.

— Women must have right to control their own fertility and equality in sexual relations

Human rights and women's rights are interwinned and based on freedom of expression.

The adopted basic principles of Beijing Commission can be achieved if we all work together for alround development of women. Otherwise the situation will not be changed. Hence we should take vow to meet the ends of justice by giving equality and equity to the women.

REFERENCES

1. Basu, D.D.; *Constitutional Law of India*, 8th Edition, Prentice Hall of India, 1991.
2. Banfia, R.K., *Indian Contract Act*, 8th Edition, Allahabad Law Agency, 1999.
3. Pandey, J.N., *Constitutional Law of India*, 27th Edition, Central Law Agency, Allahabad, 1994.
4. Nayak, S.K., *Crimes Against Women and Harijan Law Safeguard them*, The Lawyer (Soveneir), 1994.
5. Das, N.K., *Indian Women and the Law*, Vol. 75, Cuttack Law House, p. 41.
6. Senapati, R.N., *Declining Sex Ratio in Orissa*, Orissa Review, September, 1992.
7. Mishra, Dr. B.N., *Social Legislature, The Girl Child*, Orissa Review, September, 1992.
8. Nayak, H.K., *Stabilisation of Population through Regional Employment*, Orissa Review, September-October, 2003.
9. Panda, S.N., *Nari Sikhyarata: Progratira Urbikami*, Utkal Prasang (Oriya), August, 1994.

10

Empowerment of Tribal Women-Still Miles to Go

(A Study on Kandhamal District of Orissa)

Govinda Chandra Panda*

Introduction

The super structure of a country is composed of so many small sub-structures. The prominent sub-structures are political, economic and social. The political structure of our country needs no further testing and re-testing in keeping the unity of the country in diversity. The political democracy of India has already passed her dark days and is becoming a bright example in preserving the democratic rights, values and governance of the country. Similarly, the country is exhibiting spectacular performances in the economic front in terms of increase in GDP and per capita income, correcting the disequilibrium in BOP, expanding the market and production base, removing the regional disparities and ameliorating poverty and unemployment at grass roots level. This has been made possible.

(i) With the introduction of new economic reforms in early 1990's for domestic and foreign investments.

(ii) With the formation of some trade and business friendly enactments to channelise the dormant resources.

* Head, Department of Economics, A.M.C.S. College, Tikabali, Kandhamal, Orissa.

(iii) With the introduction of some new orders in institutional arrangements to modernise the tribal, rural and semi-urban economies.

(iv) By re-designing the structural set-up in relation to bring improvements in basic infrastructure.

(v) With the implementation of pro-poor polices to reduce the economic gaps of all kinds.

In a nut-shell, India today is striving out into the modern world with all economic and political capacities. Similarly, we are looking ahead towards formation of a civic and a just society based on holistic principles. But while we look ahead, we should not forget the concept of "social justice" in a broad social spectrum. Mere economic and political achievements should not and must not be considered as a single factor to determine the quality and status of human beings. There are hundreds of millions of negations and constraints in ensuring the maxim of social justice in Indian society. The presence of social exclusions also reflects the less attention of the policy planners to bring reforms in social structure. The situations clearly demonstrate that reforms in social sector in India have so far been half touched. The concepts of social justice and social exclusion are complex phenomenon and have many dimensions to be addressed.

But this research write-up intends to study only the magnitude of unequal treatment to women and gender bias while ensuring social justice to them.

Social Injustice and Social Exclusion to Women: Some Realities

Historically, we find women have been kept in the bottom rung of the ladder in terms of socio-economic development. They are the missing links in the chain of economic emancipation, political modernisation and social acculturation. Rigidly defined religious laws, some traditional barriers like the custom of veil (ghunghat), the practice of keeping women in domestic servitude and the male dominance psychology itself have left now crores of innocent women disadvantaged, vulnerable, impoverished and segregated from the main-stream of social justice. Even, the women today show less out-ward exposition in determining their own quality of life in the matters of house-hold management. In spite of some serious attempts taken before, during and immediately after independence to liberate women from inhuman exploitations, they are still miles away even to reach nearer to the point of a respectable survival.

So, it is quite imperative to examine the problems of gender discrimination in general and denial of education to tribal girl child in particular so as to formulate a holistic approach to empower women socially, politically, economically, psychologically and attitudinally. Similarly, it is also quite pertinent to focus the problems of tribal women and tribal girl child who are living amidst poverty, ill health and inadequate infrastructure facilities

Profile of the District and the Block under Study

The district of Boudh-Kandhamal was first formed on 1st January 1948. Later on this district was called as Phulbani district. After 1.4.1994 with the creation of Boudh district the popularly known Phulbani district has been re-christened as the Kandhamal district, aptly so because this mountain terrain is mainly inhabited by kandhas.

The district of Kandhamal is a centrally located district and lies in between 80° 30′ to 84° 35′ East Longitudes and 19° 34′ to 20° 34′ North Latitudes. The total geographical area of the district is 7650 sq kms and constitutes 4.91 per cent of the state's total geographical area . The forest coverage of the district is 9.82 per cent of the total forest of the state. The climate is sub-tropical in nature, hot and dry in summer , dry and cold in winter. The temperature varies from maximum of 45-degree celsius to a minimum of 0-degree celsius.

The district is predominantly inhabited by Scheduled Tribes. They constitute 51.98 per cent to the district total population (2001 census). Kandhas are the principal Scheduled Tribes found in the district followed by Gondas. Some of the primitive tribes like Kutia Kandhas, Dongria Kandhas and Mahila Kandhas are found in the remote hill areas of the district. The kandhas, by nature ,are rigid in their ethno-cultural life style and hardly welcome acculturation. Tikabali block which is under study also exhibits the same topography and climate like the district. The demography picture shows the high dominance of Kandhas in the block.

Objectives

In this backdrop attempts have been made in this chapter to explore the following objectives.

1. To study the disproportionate approach and unequal treatment to women in various sectors of activities in India.
2. To demonstrate the constraints of tribal women in the era of Economic Reforms and Social Transition.
3. To highlight some socio-economic and other indicators causing denial of primary education to tribal girl child.
4. To suggest some measures for further policy paradigms.

Methodology

Keeping in view of the objectives of the study, the Tikabali Block in the district of Kandhamal (Orissa) has been selected purposively due to its high tribal concentration. But the findings of the study can also be generalised to other parts of the Country with the similar background. For this purpose, helps have been taken from secondary sources such as journals, magazines and reports to study the negations in ensuring social justice to women in India. Similarly, the problems of tribal women have been studied on the basis of secondary sources of information. But, to examine the factors leading to denial of education to tribal girl child, data are collected from the primary sources. Accordingly, 130 parents are selected on the basis of simple random sampling method and interviewed to collect their views and opinions. Questionnaire method and group discussions have been adopted during the interview. Besides the above methods, observation method has also been adopted during the investigation . Statistical devices like mean and percentage have been used to infer conclusions.

Analysis

This section intends to examine the whole research write-up in three major parts. Statistical facts and figures have been extensively used to study gender bias in India.

Part-I attempt to highlight the negations in ensuring social justice to women in India with some statistical facts and figures.

Part-II which is the core of this write up outlines the position of the tribal women in general and the socio-economic and other indicators leading to denial of primary education to tribal girl child in particular based on the opinions collected from 130 tribal parents.

Part-III deals with the findings, suggestions and concluding remarks for further policy paradigms.

PART–1

Gender Bias and Unequal Treatment to Women: Some Truths

This part of the study exclusively deals to demonstrate the degree and magnitude of discrimination and unequal treatment to women in India. The statistical facts and figure clearly depict the negation of "social justice" to women in a broad economic, political, social and judicial set-up.

- Women constitute half of the world's population, perform nearly two-thirds of its work, receive one-tenth of the world's income and own less then one-hundredth of world's property. (UN Development Report 1980).
- Women spend two-thirds of their working hours on un-paid works but men spend just a fourth (Human Development Report 1995).
- Women work 12 hours more in a week then man (Human Development Report 1995).
- An ILO study finds that men tend to spend 60 per cent of their income in their home and 40 per cent on themselves, where as a women 90 per cent of her income on her family and 10 per cent on herself.
- The worrying problem of missing sex-women to men—is falling abnormally. Now it stands as 933 females per 1000 males (2001 census).
- 108 girl child are born against 100 boy child in spite of girl child foeticides. But in the survival point women inequality begins at birth, with 109.5 male live births per 100 female live births (1991 census).

- The literacy position also goes against ensuring justice to women in India. As per 2001 census the male literacy rate is 75.85 per cent and female is 54.16 per cent.
- Denial of education to girl child is more in comparison with male child. The drop out rate for girl is 68.38 per cent for classes I-VII as against 59.38 per cent for boys (Ministry of HRD, Govt. of India 1993).
- In the field of education, data show a disproportionate participation of women in various levels of education.
  - Primary Education—34.15 per cent
  - Middle education—36.28 per cent
  - Secondary and Higher Secondary Education—33.15 per cent
  - Higher Education—below 15 per cent
- Women representation in leading services also shows a dismal picture.
  - Indian Administrative Service—9.9 per cent
  - Indian Police Service—2.21 per cent
  - Supreme Court Judge—1 out of 25 judges (1996)
  - High Court Judges—3 per cent
  - Parliament Seats—49 (in 1999)
  - State Legislatures—2 per cent to 8 per cent since independence
  - Charted Accountants—5.8 per cent (in 1995)
  - Registered Medical Practitioners—20.8 per cent
  - Women entrepreneurs—10 per cent
- The latest data available so far reflect that women graduate seeking employments is 37.30 per cent (in rural areas) and 21 per cent (in urban areas) as against 14.98 per cent of women in rural and 7.48 per cent of men in urban area.
- Women are still deprived to participate in large numbers in Panchayati Raj Institutions except their mandatory reservation of one-third seats.

- Grama Panchayatas—40 per cent
- Panchayata Samiti—33.75 per cent
- Zilla Parisadas—32.28 per cent

(Compiled by Dept. of Rural Development Govt. of India)

- Women's employment in Central Govt., main and quasi sectors, is 9.3 per cent and 12.7 per cent respectively.
- In State Govt.'s also the employment of women in quasi sector is 7.6 per cent.
- Merely 5.9 per cent of women are engaged in house-hold sectors as low paid workers or marginal workers (1991 census).
- The work force participation for women in rural areas is estimated at 32.8 per cent and at 15.5 per cent in urban areas whereas the corresponding figures for men are higher (1994).
- The percentage of employment of women to total employment— Agriculture, 36 per cent; Industry, 12.42 per cent; Service, 19.7 per cent; (2001 census).
- 70 per cent of female labour force in rural areas is illiterate as against 43.7 per cent of males. In urban areas the proportions are 40.5 per cent (males) and 17.9 per cent (females) 1994.
- A sample survey conducted in 1991 reveals that only 13 per cent of women with land owning fathers have inherited land as daughters. In case of widows it is 49 per cent: still 51 per cent of widows are deprived to inherit land.
- On criminal grounds also women are becoming the innocent victims. The data available so that:
  - Annually on an average police registers
  - Nearly 5000 cases of dowry death
  - Nearly 30000 cases of dowry harassments

The number of cases of deserted women and divorce by mutual consent (often forced) is going up. It is estimated that more then 500000 cases of deserted women are pending in various courts for maintenance.

- Nearly 12000 cases of rapes.
- Nearly 13000 cases of kidnapping.
- Nearly 26000 cases of molestation.
- Nearly 11000 cases of sexual harassment.
- Number of cases pending trial in courts on women crimes as on 1.1.98 is 43.96 lakhs.
- Non-officially the numbers may be three times more than the actual figures.

PART–II

In this section attempts have been made to present the study in three sub-parts. Sub-part I deals with the problems of tribal economy and tribal women in general. Sub-part II intends to examine the factors leading to denial of education to tribal girl child. Sub-part III exhibits the findings of this section.

The Problems of Tribal Economy and Tribal Women in General

The State of Orissa is the second largest home for tribes next to Madhya Pradesh. The Schedule Tribes population of Orissa was 70.32 lakhs (1991 Census) which constitute 22.21 per cent of the total population of the state and 10.38 per cent of the countries total population. There are 62 Tribal communities including 12 primitive tribal groups living in the State (Tripathy 2004).

But historically we find a vulnerable group of people mainly the Scheduled Tribes have been either deprived of or denied even to enjoy the fundamental human rights. They are the most disadvantaged class of people living in the lowest strata of Indian economy. They are leading a sub-human life in their own world of despair, disrespect, derailment and dehumanization. They are the forest dwellers and the original inhabitations (Adivasi) of the soil. It has been observed that they are yet to be assimilated in the main body of the population and have remained primitive or backward with their separate entity. Ethno-culturally there is a wide range of variations among the tribal groups because of varied geographical, environmental and social life styles. But, they exhibit a close similarity in economic front. Thus, in the threshold of survival they have been politically discriminated, economically subjugated, morally humiliated, culturally isolated, socially ostracized, physically oppressed and relegated from developmental main-stream. In an environment, where the ground realities of the tribal hinterland and the tribes are in a deplorable situation, it is needless to imagine a better future for tribal women.

"The plight of tribal women is multi-magnitude in nature. They have to suffer two curses, one of being a women and another of being a tribe". The economics status of women in tribal regions is also not encouraging. Their works are not rightly appreciated because their economic contributions are always under valued. Hence, they have either been denied or discriminated from their economic rights. In primitive tribal society women are domesticated merely to bearing and rearing children, performing household chores and collecting minor forest products. Women are not treated as visible partners in the economic life of the tribal societies. They play a secondary role in house-hold decision making process and remain complete out of the socio-economy safety net. They have been deprived from self-respect and subjugated into existence at the whim and mercy of their counterparts. Consequently, women in tribal areas have been virtually sidelined in the process of economic upliftment and social reconstruction. They remain in disadvantaged positions and come completely under the grip of poverty. Social taboos also prevent the tribal women to adjust themselves in the matters of occupational mobility and structural diversification. In the context of human resource development and human capital management they are legging behind and living amidst poverty. Some market friendly enactments have also forced the tribal women to loose their intellectual property right over traditional techniques. The problems of alienation of agricultural land by the non-tribes and money lenders further aggravate the economic status of the tribal women. High consumerism and excessive commercial use of forest have resulted in first shrinking of forest resources in tribal regions thereby leading to a deplorable economic environment for the tribal women. Further, the economic reforms of early 1990s and introduction of capital intensive technologies in manufacturing and construction activities have affected the socio-economic life of the tribal women adversely in the field of exposure to various developmental schemes.

Denial of Primary Education to Tribal Girl Child

Serious efforts have been made in this section to examine the drop out problems among the tribal girl child at primary level of education and to find out the socio-economic causes leading to drop outs on the basis of the opinions of the parents . Accordingly, to get information and statistics one "dropout problems enquiry schedule" for the parents has been prepared by the investigator. The "dropout problems enquiry schedule" has been depicted below. The responses of the parents have been shown in percentage value in the findings.

Dropout Problems Enquiry Schedule

Sl. No	*Socio-economic & other indicators Causing dropouts*
1.	Illiterate and ignorant parents
2.	Poverty and economic problems
3.	Nature of The tribal life (settled, semi-settled, practising shifting cultivation, migratory)
4.	No gain from education
5.	Size of the family
6.	Discouraging school administration and environment
7.	Cultural barriers (assimilated tribes, tribes in transitions and primitive tribes
8.	Domestics and house-hold economic use of the children
9.	Staff pattern
10.	Difficult communication

Findings of the Study in Inter-linking with the Views of the Parents

To draw the findings, responses of the parents have been expressed in percentage values. Their views have been collected mostly on the basis of personal interview, group discussion and observation methods. Nearly 75 per cent of the parents are of the opinion that the root cause of girl drop out is the prevailing illiteracy and ignorance. Even after intensive literacy drive more than 60 per cent of the tribal fathers and 75 per cent of the tribal mothers are still illiterates. 80 per cent of the parents believe that poverty and economic backwards are main hurdles to provide education to girl child. It is visualise that economical poor parents prefer to provide education to boy child rather than girl child. They usually employ their girl child in informal sector like agriculture and construction as labourers. Nature of tribal life also determines the access to education by the girls in tribal region. The percentage of opinions are the parents in case of settled, semi-settled, practising shifting cultivation and migratory tribal life are 20 per cent, 40 per cent, 58 per cent and 73 per cent respectively. Almost 57 per cent of the parents view that present education are useless and has no link with employment. So, they rather want to keep some amount of money towards meeting the dowry cost of their girls in stead of investing in education. The status of education of girl child also depends upon the size of the family. 37 per cent of parents opinion that more is the number of members in the family less is the opportunity for the girls to get admitted in the schools. 47 per cent of parents argue that ill-designed curriculum, loose administration, unsuitable school environment, inadequate hostel facility, lack of government incentives, insufficient class rooms and teachers are some of the secondary reasons to deny education to tribal girl child. No doubt some awareness about education has increased in rural tribal masses but the habitual inhibition and family imperatives still thwart the attempts to send their girl child regularly to schools and for this 37 per cent are the parents believe that cultural constraints are the main obstacles. Tribes in primitiveness are culturally more rigid than the tribes in assimilation and transition. In this connection early marriage and fear for acculturation are the important reasons. 27 per cent of the parents respond that the reason for drop out of girl child are their participation in domestic and household activities like looking after the younger kids, collecting minor forest products, fuels, fodders and water for the family. They are also engaged in activities like cattle rearing, grazing, poultry and selling fire woods in daily markets. They think bread first and education next. Staff pattern also influences the position of girl education. Schools where more lady teachers are serving the parents

(22%) choose to send their girl child. Their argument is they have no faith upon the male teachers on the ground that their grown-up may be sexually abused. The last indicator which hinders (12%) girl education is difficult communication facilities and unfair behaviours of the strangers while the girls are on the way to the schools.

Suggestions and Concluding Remarks

A perusal of the study clearly acknowledges that gender discrimination is one of the most pervading forms of institutionalised deprivation and there is need to rectify the situation. It is mainly because of unabated poverty, unwieldy unawareness, inaccessible illiteracy, uncontrollable population growth and dreaded cultural beliefs. So empowerment of women including the tribal women should not and must not be considered as a separate and technical exercise altogether. We have done much in this path by conferring powers to women in judicial and legislative platforms. What rightly needed is "empowerment to women". So, instead of talking about empowerment of women the debate should be on empowerment of women. What is women empowerment? Terminologically, it is wrong and self-contradictory. But, methodologically it is a conceptual approach. Empowerment does mean automatic process of acquiring powers. It implies women needs to acquire power by her self. The dangers of loss of powers imply empowerment. Powers already existed and can not be lost and separated imply empowerment. This can be realised only beyond our existing institutional arrangements. The existing arrangements have so far done nothing or a little to empower women. Hence the issue is the discussion should begin on women equality rather than on women inequality that is the only way out for empowerment of women. Men are in empowerment from birth. That should be the psychology towards women empowerment both at domestic and societal level. Empowerment means nothing to be given everything should be there; the task is just to acquire. All these need, "a natural bend of mind set" of women in the games power exercises. That is the real and institutional process of women empowerment and power polarisation in favour of women in a society. So in the whole issue of women equality, empowerment is possible partly by gender sensitisation and partly by:

1. Women in Development (WID)
2. Women and Development (WAD)
3. Gender and Development (GAD)

To achieve these objectives purely new women specific economic institutions should be created with realistic outlooks. In judicial and legislative platforms necessary provisions should be made in the constitution for setting of special courts not only to speed of the pending cases but also to impose heavy punishments for any kind of women offences in future. The situations are quite worse in tribal regions. If the planners ever want to liberate the tribal women the foremost task should be to emancipate them from the clutches of poverty and illiteracy. Illiteracy is a big concern in tribal region. The literacy position of tribal women is 20 per cent. Similarly the rate of dropout of tribal girl child for the classes I-VII is 74 per cent (daily Oriya news Prajatantra). Hence attempts should be made at all levels Govt., Non-Govt. and Voluntary to check dropouts by creating widespread awareness about the social importance of education in general and the girl child in particular. Education should not be seemed as an investment in a vacuum rather it should be viewed as production of high quality inputs for various socio-economic and political exercises. It is a holistic approach in the matters of human resource management and planning. As a part of institutional approach HEEA (Habitation Elementary Education Authority) should function effectively. In tribal regions, the HEEA can take in the from of:

- Parent-teacher committee
- Mother- teacher association
- A school management committee or, a hamlet education committee

The Panchayati Raj Institutions (PRIs) in accordance with Panchayat Extension Scheduled Area (PESA) Act should participate in the process of primary education as a supreme guardian. HEEA shall report to LEEA (Local Elementary Education Authority) in the matters of administration and dropout. SCERT in collaboration with DIET should actively impart methodological training to the Block Level Resource (BRC) persons to mobilise the parents not to withdraw the girl child from the school. Swechhasebi Sikhya

Sahayaks (SSS) should also be engaged for social mobilisation of primary education in favour of tribal girl child as a part of SSA (Sarba Sikhya Abhijan). Similarly the UNICEF financed projects like Comprehensive Access to Primary Education (CAPE) and Early Childhood Education (ECE) can go a long way in improving the situations in tribal regions. To conclude, all these efforts, if done sincerely, may bring some realities in fulfilling our commitments of Free and Compulsory Education (FACE) up to elementary levels of education, Universalisation of Primary Education (UPE) and Total Literacy (TL) by 2010 A.D.

REFERENCES

1. Tripathy, S.N. "*Education for Tribal Women*" in Self Edited Tribal Women in India, Mohit Publication, New Delhi, 2002.
2. Panda, G.C. "*Development of Tribal Women through Self-Help Groups: A Study in Kandhamal District*" , Paper Presented in an UGC National Conference (8-10 August 2004), Nagarjuna Univeristy, Guntur, AP.
3. Panda, G.C. "*Empowering Tribal Women through SHGs: A Study in Kandhamal District*" Paper Presented in an UGC State Level Conference (12-13 Sept. 2004), UNS College, Khairabad, Mugpal, Jajpur, Orissa.
4. Panda, G.C. and Tripathy, Dr. S. "*Impact of Road Transport on Population : A Study in Kandhamal District, Orissa.*" in "Problems of Population in India" Edited by Panigrahy, R.L., Discovery Publishing House, New Delhi, 2004. (in Press).
5. Smaranika Kandhamala Mohouchhaba 2003 : District Council of Culture, Kandhamal District, Phulabani.
6. District Statistical Handbook Kandhamal-1999: Directorate of Economics and Statistics, Govt. of Orissa, Bhubaneswar.
7. Sharma, K.R. "*A Study of Educational Backwardness of Tribal Students*", The Educational Quarterly, April 1983.
8. Panda G.C. "*Panchayati Raj Institution and Tribal Development—A Study in Kandhamal*", Paper Presented in a National Seminar at SRTM University, Nanded, Jan. 24-25.
9. Mahajan Sumitra. An article, "*Philosophy, Goals and Achievement*," Yojna Vol. 45, Aug. 2001.
10. Manohar, Sujata. An article "*How Effective are the Laws*"? Yojna Vol. 45, Aug. 2001.
11. Kukreti, B.R. and Saxena, M. An article "*Drop out Problems Among Tribal Students at School Level: A Case Study*" Kurukshetra, Vol. 52, No. 11, Sept. 04.

11

Women Empowerment in Nation-building

Dr. Bishnu Narayan Sethy

Nation building is a complex and multi-dimensional process signifying the political will enunciated through properly formulated development policies. Economic, education and social infrastructures are needed to enhance the capability and provide opportunity to each individual to realize his fullest potential. Human development with the underlying goal of improved human happiness and quality of life constitutes the core component of nation-building process.

Just as the UNESCO constitutions preamble opens with the magnificent words so often quoted "since war begins in the minds of men that the defense of peace must be constructed" the process of nation-building must begin from the minds and hearts of the people. This process does not call for a doctrinaire approach—it would certainly call or an approach based on feeling of good will, equity and oneness. Equally important would be to face the challenges of force of counterveiling this approach representing fissiparous tendencies, centrifugal and divisive forces and sectarian outlook.

Nationalism all through the history of mankind has been one of the most powerful urges that moves a people. It is around this feeling of nationalism that cluster sentiments and traditions and a sense of common living and common purpose. National consciousness is a pre-requisite and a determining factor for national unity. National unity to a very large extent, would depend upon one's perception and conception of nation.

To the German mind, the word nation conveys, fascinating nuances and connotations. It conveys the impression of a great powerful and highly civilized people with its own state and the word national is employed only for such lofty concepts in national hour, national unity, the national flag. In Barke's view nation is not merely a multitude of human beings living together. But a historical personality with a specific political and social structure, united by a sort of tacit consent and guide by a small class trained in politics, public service and embodying the national traditions. Frederick Hertz in his similar study, Nation in History and Politics (1966), points out to the widespread modern usage of nation identities a nation with a people constituted as a state. In his view every state forms a nation and every citizen is a member of the nation. This definition of course exclusively legal one. Many states were or are composed of different nationality. The Scots, the welsh and the Irish regard themselves as nations, though they live in a common state with the English. Therefore, in modern history the moving force is not the legal concept of nationality but, the social and emotional force of national consciousness.

Nationalism, inspite of the recent events in several part of the world, involving ethnic and ideological conflicts is still universal in its influence and appeal. The nationalist ideal, by and large, in most of the countries is deep and strong. The abiding appeal of nationalism to the spirit of man has to be recognized and respected. The concept of nationalism is not the product of one age, nation, class, party, religion or philosophy, but that each his partly contributed to its growth, partly counteracted it, though in different degrees.

It has been repeated stated that one of the prime goal of most developing nation is to create a sense of national identity witl.in a society often composed of desperate ethnic, tribal and linguistic segments. Although militant nationalism leading to hostility between nations can be deplored, few questions the value of integrating and inter-connecting in co-operative fashion the diverse cultures and interests within a society.

Several tendencies and attitudes have been attributed to nation and nationalism and different elements: cultural, linguistic or even religious have been emphasized by different parties on different occasions and in different contexts. It is however accepted that, by and large nationalism represents ardent love of people, unrelenting fight for its true interests, protection against foreign interference and aggression, safe -guarding its traditions and stressing national unity and solidarity and of course, sub-ordination of particular interest to those of nation.

Nationalism or national consciousness is complex and abstract. Nationalism is a set of mind. It is the result of social learning. This feeling of national consciousness could be generated only over a period of time, overcoming large number of obstacles and barriers, vested interest and countervailing influences. National unity by definition, is a national objective. It can not be confined to particular groups or classes of people—whether social, religious, economic, political or intellectual. Its objectives has necessarily to be a super person or national character which transcends and binds together people of every type, profession, region, creed, caste or race in the country into a single identifiable whole.

Empowerment of Women

Since women constitutes almost half of the population of the country, efforts at nation building would have to take into consideration, in full major and perspective, the role and the contribution of women in this noble task of national development.

The movement for the empowerment of the women as a part of major civilization transformation has been one of the significant social and political developments of the closing decades or the twentieth century.

The Road Travelled-from Welfare to Empowerment

In India numerous steps have been undertaken to provide constitutional safeguards and institutional frameworks for activities pertaining to women welfare. The development of women has been the central focus in developmental planning since independence. There have been various shifts in policy approaches during the last twenty years from the concept of welfare in the 1970s to development in 1980s and now to empowerment in the 1990s, now the emphasis is on the inclusion of women in decision-making and their participation at the policy formulation levels.

Empowerment has been variously understood as a process, a movement, a collective action, etc. In the area of the land rights of women, where the term carries economic significance, eminent economists Vina Agarwal defines "empowerment as a process that enhance the ability of disadvantaged and powerless individuals or group of challenge and change in their favour, existing power relationship that places them in sub-ordinate economic, social and political positions. Empowerment can manifest itself in acts of individual resistence as well as in group mobilization".

The concept of empowerment has been equated by some with collective action. However, this definition of empowerment thus would appear too narrow. In a limited sense, collective action may itself empower women by enhancing their self confidence and their ability and willingness to challenge oppression, but in a large sense it means empowerment, where in empowerment lies not only in the process of challenging gender inequality but in eliminating it.

The advancement of women, including the right-freedom of thought, conscience, religion and belief, contribute to the moral, ethical, spiritual and intellectual needs of women as well as men, individually or in the community. It also guarantees the possibility of realizing their full potential in society and shopping their lives in accordance with their own aspirations.

Empowerment of women implies process by which women's power to self organization is promoted and reinforced. They develop the capacity for self-reliance act crossing the relationship of subordination on account of gender, social and economic status and the role in the family and society. It encompasses their ability to make cherishes, control resources and enjoy participatory relationship within family and community. To achieve these objectives empowerment of women also implies their ability to participate in and also lead social movement to remove obstacles in their progress towards their goal.

Institutional Framework

Besides providing a number of constitutional safeguards the government has created an effective institutional framework to strengthen the movement for women empowerment.

Role of Department of Women and Child Development

A separate Department of Women and Child Development was set up in 1985 as a part of the Ministry of Human Resource Development (HRD) to give the required impetus to the Development of Women and Children. The department in its nodal capacity formulates plans, policies and programmes and enacts and amends legislation and coordinates the efforts of both governmental and non-governmental organisations working to improve the lot of women and children in the country.

The national policy for empowerment of women is being finalised by the department. The policy would prescribe strategies and action points to bridge the gap between the equal de-jure status and unequal de-facto position of women in the country. It would seek to guide action at every level and in every sector by main-streaming gender perspectives into all laws, policies, programmes, regulations and budgetary allocation of the government.

The department is in the process of setting up a National Resource Centre for Women. This would be a nodal body to implement policies and programmes for women by training, policy support, information, dissemination, research and documentation.

Role of National Commission for Women

In pursuance of the National Commission for Women Act 1990, the National Commission for Women was set up on 31st January 1992, the functions assigned to the commission are wide and varied covering almost all facts relating to safeguarding women's right and promotion of empowerment. The commission has a chairman, five members and a member secretary, all nominated by the central government. The commission continues to pursue its mandated activities: review of legislation, intervention in specific individual complaints of atrocities, denial of rights and sexual harassment at place of work. Remedial action to safeguard the interest of women is suggested to the appropriate authorities. The commission has accorded highest priority to securing speedy justice to women. The commission also organizes Parivarik Mahila Lok Adalatas, offering counselling in family disputes and conducting training programmes for creating legal awareness among women.

Women and Development

According to the report of the world conference of the UN Decade for women Copenlnogen, July 1980: while women represent 50 per cent of the world adult population and one third of official labour force, they perform nearly two thirds of all working hours, receive only a tenth of world income and own less than one per cent of the world property. This is more than true of India. Despite developmental planning, and the special status accorded to women in the Indian constitution, there has not been a substantial qualitative improvement in the position of a largea majority of woman living in rural areas.

The status of women can also be viewed from a development perspective. Development as defined nby the world conference of jthe UN Decade for woman is interpreted to mean total development including development in the political economic, social, cultural and other dimensions of human life as also the physical moral, intellectual and cultural growth of the human person. Women development should not only be viewed as an issue in social development but should be seen as an essential component in every dimension of development.

In this context it would be note worthy to recall the observations of Noble Laureate Amartya Sen in his book—India-Economic Development and Social Opportunity: Women's empowerment can positively influence the lives not only of women themselves but also of men, and of course those of children. There is much evidence for instance, that women's education tends to reduce child mortality rates, for both boys and girls. In fact there is good reason to relate the remarkable high life expectancy levels in Kerala to its educational achievement, particularly of women and on the other side, to relate the low life expectancies of some of the northern states to backwardness in female education. The subordination of woman, in Indian Society tends to impair their effectiveness in reducing deprivation in general and it is not only the well-being of female children or adult women which is improved by the enhanced agency of women.

Judicial and Constitutional Measures

An eminent writer a gender and development subjects, Dr. Sarala Gopalan a former secretary, Government of India in her contribution an Empowerment of women, enumerates several judicial and constitutional measures taken to further the cause of women Empowerment. Some of the steps enumerated are:

1. The Indian Succession Act 1952 subsequently modified in 1997 concerning interstate and testamentary succession as applicable to non-Hindus, for example, Christians, Parsis etc. doesn't recognize women's right to succession. However in the famous Mary Roy's case, the Supreme Court recognized women's right to interstate and testamentary succession.
2. In 1997 , the Supreme Court ratified guidelines against sexual harassment at work place in a significant judgement in a writ petition for enforcement of fundamental rights of working women. The court held that sexual harassment at work place would be violative of Article 19, which guarantees right to practice any profession, trade or business, that the right to work is dependant upon a safe working environment and right to life with dignity.
3. The Supreme Court in 1999 recognised the natural and unconditional guardianship of the mother in the context of legal challenge of excusive guardianship of the father under the relevant guardianship law.

Likewise the 73rd and 74th Constitutional Amendments mark a watershed in the field of advancement of Indian women as they ensure one-third of total seats for women in all elected offices of local bodies, in both rural and urban areas. According to government of India Beijing report 1995, this provides an opportunity to about one million rural women to emerge as leader/decision makers at the grassroot level and ever public life through the existing 0.25 million bodies.

It can be conclusively stated that there has been a radical change in the movement for women empowerment. Recognition is dawning that women are indeed becoming a political force, both nationally and internationally. Since women rights have been accepted as human rights at the international; level, the movement for empowerment is burned together strength. Once the rights are proclaimed, the process of empowerment cannot stop. The rights move to the top of political agenda. However, doubts have been expressed at several for a, including in the report of the Independent commission on population and quality of life about the danger of empowerment being sloganised without coming realization. There is even danger that empowerment may become devoid of meaning, if, effective steps are not taken to implement various administrative and constitutional measures.

In a country like India with strong tradition of democratic functioning, a vibrant public opinion and influential section of society interested in progress and welfare of women, the movement for women's empowerment is bound together strength. Such a powerful onward thrust towards strengthening this movement is bound to make major contribution toward nation building.

REFERENCES

1. Swasti, M.: *Women in Knowledge Societies, A Keynote Address*, Global Knowledge Forum, Malaysia, 2000.
2. India 2003 Reference Annual, Publication Division, Ministry of I & B, Govt. of India.
3. Nath, V.E.: ICT Enabled Knowledge Societies for Human Development. Information Technology in Developing Countries, Vol. 10, No. 2, August; 2000.
4. Employment News, September-1996, October-1997, June-1998, May, 2000.

12

Women Empowerment in Policy and Politics

R.N. Panigrahy

Women constitute half of the population of India i.e. 407.1 million according to the 1991 census report and it is sure that there cannot be any development unless they are empowered to fulfil their needs and interests. Women as a motherhood of the nation should be strong, aware and alert mother with child is the future of the nation.

Empowerment of women for effective participation at various levels in Panchayati Raj Institutions (PRIs) has been discussed and debated from 1957 onwards. The first concrete measure to the constitutional sanction to it, was taken by Mr. Rajiv Gandhi Government by introducing 64th Constitutional Amendment Bill on Local Government on 15th May, 1989. It was defeated by small margin in Rajaya Sabha.

Mr. Narasimha Rao government has successfully enacted the 73rd Constitutional Amendment Act, 1992 which included 29 items for strengthening PRIs at all level. The Act is extremely vested for political empowerment of women, SCs, STs. Not less than one-third i.e. 33% of the total membership of Panchayat bodies has been reserved for women including SCs and STs. These seats may be allocated by rotation to different constituencies in a Panchayat body. Perhaps, India is the first country recognising this social status and to have taken concrete measures to draw women into leadership positions and thereby into politics by giving them one-third reservation. This ample opportunity have created far reaching consequences in Indian politics and social life. We cannot make democracy meaningful without the full involvement of women in every sphere.

Traditionally, women are considered to be weak and inferior to men. Women suffer from a lower self-esteem because of social subjugation and lack of economic independence. Due to such a societal status of women, Simon de Beauvoir stated "One is not born a women: one becomes a women. No biological, psychological or economic destiny can determine how the human female will appear in the society". In view of this, reservation of one-third seats to Panchayats for them is a silent revolution to improve their status.

Our country has made a legislative expediency over political initiatives in ensuring participation of women at the grassroot level politics by providing mandatory reservation into local bodies as per 73rd and 74th Constitutional Amendment Acts. Article 15(3) makes a special provision, enabling the state to make affirmative discrimination in favour of women. Article 51(A) renounces practices derogatory to the dignity of women. Under section 243(D) clauses 1, one-third seats in the three tiers of Panchayats and Municipalities are specifically reserved for women including SCs and STs. One-third of presidential positions in the three-tiers of panchayats and municipalities will also go to women leaders. This has a salutary effect on the political empowerment of women as it will be from among them that the future leaders of the nation will emerge.

Women constitute at least half of the voters, in all countries and exercise their rights to vote in near proportion to men, but in political offices it has not grown in equal proportion even now. The depository between women and men participation in political, civil, social and economic shares can be attributed to socially constructed gender roles rather than biological differences so, constitution of India granted equality of women to men under Article 14, on rights and opportunities in the political economic and social spheres.

Voting is the most basic level of political participation. Political participation ensures changes in Government's behaviour, better response to citizen's needs, reframing from arbitrary, intensive and coercive exercise of power over individual by the state machinery. It can also bring change of attitude among citizens by solving their conflict with the govt. and allowing them to exercise vigilance over Govt. affairs.

Spreading legal literacy among the community generally and elected representatives particularly is another measure that can accelerate women's political participation in equal opportunity of men. The mandatory provision of reservation for women in local Govts. should follow increased awareness generation as to their roles and responsibilities as members among the elected representatives. They must be properly trained and empowered to exercise their authority in the democratic bodies and among public, in accordance with the values of democracy. The poor record of political participation of women and their absence in the decision making bodies make the enforcement of many social legislations aimed at gender equality on unfinished social task. Increasing participation of women in politics enhances lobbying power over public affairs and that will in turn result in their power over private life also.

Government Intervention for Women's Empowerment

Till women are empowered the nation will not be full-fledged. In the 4th World Conference on Women in Beijing in 1995, the US First Lady Hilari Clinton has strongly asserted the link between human rights and women rights quote. "It is time for us to say here in Beijing and the world to here that it is no longer acceptable to discuss women's rights as separate from human rights". She said "It is a violation of human rights when babies are denied food or drowned or suffocated or their spines broken, simply because they are born girls. When women are raped in their own communities as a tactic or prize of war, when women die due to domestic violence, when young girls are brutalised by the painful practice of right to plan their own families and are forced to have abortions or are sterilised against their will, these are violations of human rights".

Considering the relevance and importance of women's development and empowerment, the Govt. of India has enacted important legislations, planned and organised several schemes and programmes aiming at promotion of the cause of women and prevention of problems of women. One among such innovative programmes is "Counselling services" for families in general and for women in particular. In counselling services three roles are central— the remedial, the preventive and the developmental.

1. The remedial role entails working with individuals or groups of girls/women to assist them in bringing remedy to the problems of one kind or another.
2. The preventive role is one in which the counsellor seeks to anticipate, circumvent and if possible forestall difficulties that may arise in the future. Preventive intervention may focus on what is called psycho-education, aiming to forestall the development of problems or events.
3. In developmental role of the counsellor is referred to as the educative and development, the purpose of which is to "help girls and women to plan, obtain and derive maximum benefits from the kinds of experiences which will enable them to discover and develop their potentialities.

The different departments/sectors involved in the implementation of these programmes, including nodal Department of Women and Child Development, Rural Development, Health and Education in India.

The major programmes in this regard are the poverty alleviation programme of IRDP, TRYSEM, where there are 40% of the benefits should go to women. In the wage employment programme of Jawahar Rojagar Yojana (JRY), Rural Landless Employment, Guarantee Programme (RLEGP), etc. 30% of the benefits have been reserved for women; these programmes are implemented by Department of Rural Development.

The programmes which were launched by Department of Women and Child Development in 1987 aimed to upgrade the skills of poor and assetless women; to provide them employment on the sustainable basis in the traditional sector of agriculture, dairy farming, fisheries, sericulture, handloom etc. for women's development. The department was set-up in 1985 as a part of Ministry of Human Resource Development (MHRD) to give the much needed impetus to the holistic development of women and children. The major policy initiatives undertaken by the Department of National Commission for Women (NCW), Rasthriya Mahila Kosh (RMK), adoption for National Nutrition Policy (NCP), strengthening of ICDS, setting up of National Credit Fund (NCF), launching of Indira Mahila Yojana (IMY), Balika Samridhi Yojana (BSY), Rural Women's Development and Empowerment Projects (RWDEP). The NORAD assisted programme by this department extends assistance to organisations to train women in the non-traditional sectors like electronics, watch assembly, computers, printing technology, beauty culture, handloom, etc. to give sustainable employment to women. The department has been implemented the pogramme "Hostels for working women" from 1973 to provide safe and cheap accommodation to single working of employment.

Socio-Economic Programme (SEP) which is implemented by Central Social Welfare Board (CSWB) to provide work and wages to needy such as destitute, widows, deserted, economically backward and handicapped.

Rashtriya Mahila Kosh (RMK) was set up in March, 1993 to extend the credit facilities to poor and needy women in the informal sector. It is a very significant intervention launched to satisfy the credit needs of poor, assetless. Women mostly in informal sector. Since its inception, it has sanctioned credit of Rs. 57.09 crores through 367 NGOs to benefit 2,77,662 women. Launched in 15th August, 1995 the scheme being implemented in 200 blocks in the country for the holistic empowerment of women. Till December 1998, 37,000 small homogenous women groups have been formed under the scheme.

The National Commission for Women (NCW), set-up in 1992 covers issues relating safeguarding women's rights and promotion of their empowerment. The Commission works for review of laws, intervention in specific individual complaints of atrocities and sexual harassment of women at work place and remedial actions to safeguard the interest of women.

The programme of STEP, launched in 1987, seeks to provide new upgraded skills to and assetless women in the traditional sectors of agriculture, sericulture, handicrafts, fisheries, diary farming, poultry etc. Different policies like National Plan of Action (NPA) 1976, National Perspective Plan (NPP) 1993, National Plan of Action for Girl Child (NPAGC) 1991-2000, National Policy on Education (NEP) 1986, National Policy on Health (NPH) 1983, National Commission Women (NCW) 1992, through National Commission Act, 1992 are the policies implemented by Government of India for the betterment of girls and women of India for their empowerment.

Conclusion

Instead of the empowerments, women representatives are ornamental in nature and political, economic, social consciousness is found lacking among them. They are affected by caste, class divisions, feudal attitudes, patriarchal nature of the family and village social environment, ethnic and religious separation and the like. The elected representatives are records only. They are not free from male.

Due to such an empowerment, the women community is not actually empowered themselves. Thus, the famous poet of India, Rabindra Nath Tagore has cried out in anguish more than half a century ago:

"O Lord, why have you not given women the right to conquer her destiny, why does she have to wait head bowed by the roadside waiting with tired patience, hoping for a miracle in the marrow."

REFERENCES

1. *"Social Welfare"*, a Monthly Magazines.

   Nov., 1995, (i) Attitude Towards Reservation for Women (p. 3-9); (ii) A Paradism Shift from Welfare (p. 26-30).

   April, 1976, (i) Child Labour Challenges and Opportunity (p. 3-4); (ii) Panchayati Raj—The Stranglehold of Golden Bias (p. 5-6); (iii) Panchayati Raj—Reservation: Boon or Bane? (p. 7-9).

2. *"Orissa Review"*, a Monthly Magazine of Orissa Govt.

   February, 1997, (i) Employment of the Common People a Noble System (p. 1-3); October, 1996, (i) Panchayati Raj and Rural Development: Some Basic Issues (p. 24-26).

3. *Employment News Weekly*, 4-10 March 2001, (i) Employment of Women, Role of the State (p. 1) by Sumitra Mahajan, Minister of State & Child Development.

4. *Kurukshetra*, a Monthly Magazine, April, 1996.

13

Empowerment of Women through Information Technology

Deepak Bishoyi*

Information Technology has become a potential force in transforming social, economic and political life globally and without its incorporation it is difficult for countries or regions to develop if not to survive. In spite of some skeptical arguments against the relevance of information technology in Indian conditions, may people are hopeful of exploiting its potential to spur not only growth in the national economy as a whole, but also to bring in new opportunities to those who are mired in despair. It is in this context, that role of information technology for women's empowerment acquires greater significance. This paper makes an attempt to analyse the various dimensions of empowerment of women through information technology. These dimensions are: Economic Empowerment, Social Empowerment, Political Empowerment, Empowerment through education, Empowerment through preservation of indigenous knowledge traditions. IT can also be effectively exploited for improving health, nutrition, reproductive health, maternity, etc.

The impact of information technology on social has not been uniformly beneficial, and the technology divide is being

---

* **Research Scholar, Department of Economics, Berhampur University, Orissa.**

increasingly felt, especially in the developing countries. Serious obstacles still continue in achieving gender equality. Cultural attitudes and gender stereotyping are impediments to education leading to more men, than women in scientific and impediments to education leading to more men, than women in scientific and technical careers and in decision making positions, thus increasing gender inequity. Equal access to science is not only a social and ethical requirement for human development, but also essential for realizing the full potential of scientific communities and for orienting scientific programmes towards meeting the needs of humankind. With women's empowerment as a key objective, they can use technology to successfully build personal confidence and self-esteem that has had wider implications in women's lives (Sharma, 2003).

Within the framework of a democratic polity, our laws, development policies, plans and programmes have aimed at women's advancement in different spheres. From the Fifth Five-Year Plan (1974-1978) onwards has been a marked shift in the approach to women's issues from welfare to development. In recent years, the empowerment of women has been recognized as the central issue in determining the status of women. The National Commission for Women was set up by an Act of Parliament in 1990 to safeguard the rights and legal entitlements of women. The 73rd and 74th Amendments (1993) to the constitute of India have provide for reservation of seats in the local bodies of Panchayats and Municipalities for women, laying a strong foundation for their participation in decision making at the local levels.

It is important for feminist and IT scholars to look not only at categories of gender as they have been defined, but also as they could be redefined and changed through the influence of IT. The appeal is clear, if we resphere our view to see the user of technology as a subject, rather than an object, we provide an avenue for women to act as agents of change (Lawley, 1993). This suggestion indicates that technological system and their effects can be viewed as a form of ideology, shaped by the designers and managers of technology who can act as user and producer at the same time. With the characteristic of interactive technology, Internet can provide women (and marginalize groups) a space to reshape their appearance and/

or identity through representations that flow from words and images. These systems allow women to break boundaries and redefine themselves outside the traditional categories of "object" or "others".

For scholars, looking through a number of websites, for instance geek girls, they will be able to make clear argument that gender is construction and technology needs not only reflect pre-existing gender, instead it can be an area for the reshaping of those marginalized categories. Furthermore, creating better representations of women in the cyberspace can help more women become comfortable users of communication technology. It will be possible for women and other marginalized groups to accomplish training and educational programmes in order to be effective user and produces of information technology.

To ensure of being a gender sensitive information society, the gender implications of technical polity areas such as code and regulation, network architecture and available, deployment and pricing, training and education, as well as consumer protection need to be taken an board and made dialogue among IT and gender policy makers. A forum that contains diverse perspective, for instance technological base, gender base, economic base and cultural base, should be provided to exchange experiences on IT strategies and identify best policy and practices, where they can learn for each other.

There are a number of important considerations along the process of development and implementation of policy making. There are:

- Making arrangements that supports universal access to IT.
- Extension of infrastructure, particularly wireless and satellite communications and other forms of public access, to rural areas and urban poor areas in places that convenient and accessible to women.
- Increasing effective collaborations with various institutions relating to IT and gender in order to ensure that the reduction of gender digital divide is addressed in all policy and strategies of government and industrial sectors.

- Empowering women's participation in IT by increasing more useful and comfortable contexts that suitable for women's everyday lives, such as health, education, family, trade, law, farming, energy resource and other women's development areas.
- Encouraging a bottom-up development model that makes communications, information and other self-help tools directly available to communities and poor women to come over their constraints. This bottom-up model requires partnership with government; NGOs and business to provide women basic practicing to use IT to meet their basic needs, develop small business connection and share experiences with other across country. The bottom up model will also empower women to take charge of their own development.
- Promoting women's participation in all levels of IT government and industrial sectors and to enhance women in these sectors with gender perspectives by providing training, forum and other forms of activities to rising gender awareness.
- Empowering women, community and NGOs or Civil Groups to form networks, link to the Internet to monitor governments and private sectors performances. Such effort can enable transparency and exercise people fundamental rights.

Economic Empowerment

Poverty Eradication: Since women comprise the majority of the population below the poverty line and are very often in situations of extreme poverty, given the harsh realities of intra-household and social discrimination, macro economic policies. Use of IT provides the poverty eradication programmes will specially address the needs and problems of such women. There will be improved implementation of programmes which are already women oriented with special targets for women. Steps will be taken for mobilization of poor women and convergence of services, by offering them a range of economic and social options, along with necessary support measures to enhance their capabilities.

Globalization: Globalization has presented new challenges for the realization of the goal of women's equality, the gender impact of which has not been systematically evaluated fully. However, from the micro-level studies that were commissioned by the Department of Women and Child Development, it is evident that there is a need for re-farming policies for access to empowerment and quality of employment. Benefits of the growing global economy have been unevenly distributed leading to wider economic disparities, the frminization of poverty, increased gender inequality through often deteriorating working conditions and unsafe working environment especially in the informal economic and rural areas. IT strategies will be designed to enhance the capacity of women and empower them to meet the negative social and economic impacts, which may flow from the globalisation process.

Agriculture: In view of the critical role of women in the agriculture and allied sectors, as producers, concentrated efforts will be made to ensure the benefits of training, extension and various programmes will reach them in proposition to their numbers. The programmes for training women in soil conservation, social forestry, dairy development and other occupations allied to agriculture like horticulture, livestock including small animal husbandry, poultry, fisheries, etc. will be expended to benefit women workers in the agriculture sectors. IT could provide women farmers, farm related information such as best package of practices, weather forecasting, access to credit, prices and availability of farm inputs, market information etc. Access to such information by women will facilitate participation of women farmer's in decision making process.

Entrepreneurship: As it is evident from the recent IT experiences, one of the most powerful application of IT is electronic commerce. This e-commerce, in the context of women's empowerment, refers not just to selling of products and services online but to the promotion of a new class of IT savvy women entrepreneurs. IT is capable of influencing the entrepreneurial behaviour of women by improving their innovativeness, decision making ability, access to various services and ability to co-ordinate the activities and people. Besides, it provides information to small business owners especially women which will be helpful in expending their horizons. Another important area is core IT sector empowerment. There are significant opportunities for women in software. Network administration, education and training, etc. are the areas of IT where can benefit enormously.

Political Empowerment

Indubitably, IT is an excellent tool to improve governance and strengthen our democracy. It is particularly powerful for generating and enhancing the political awareness among the women, who hitherto have been isolated and were without a voice. The IT will make democracy real. Complete access to required information free consolation with the people and unhindered communication channels will be the key to political power of women.

73rd Constitutional Amendment Act has, no doubt, brought a million women to public space for the first time. Experiences from the field show that majority of these women elected representatives have limited knowledge of their authorities and responsibilities. Women's use of IT can abolish their isolation and informed citizens, to communicate and to expand their range of vision. More they get objective information, more will be there participation. In turn more participation lead to political empowerment.

Using IT, women can have access to government information such as rules and regulations, provision available for the women, policies, administrative and online services, etc. Another area of interest is online discussion among the women regarding wide range of topics, which can influence the women's empowerment. The initiative of self-employed women's association (SEWA) is worth mentioning in this discussions through Panchayati Raj where by rural women pose questions that are answered promptly by a panel of experts. Through translation modules, responses go to the women in their vernacular languages (Meera and Rao, 2003).

Social Empowerment

Education: The single most important factor in improving the ability of girls and women are to take advantage of information technology in education. Information technology can be used both for formal and non-formal education. Education for empowerment means women gaining an understanding and control over social, economic and political forces in over to improve their standing in society.

Health

Women's use of IT can know the problem of both nutrition and health services which will be adopt and special attention will be given to the needs of women and the girl at all stages of the life cycle. The reduction of infant mortality and maternal mortality, which are sensitive indicators of human development, is a priority concern, women should have access to comprehensive, affordable and quality health care, measures will be adopted that take into account the reproductive rights of women to enable them to exercise informed choice, their vulnerability to sexual and health problems together with endemic, infectious and communicable diseases such as malaria, T.B. and water borne diseases. The social development and health consequences of HIV/AIDS and other sexually Transmitted Diseases (STD) will be tackled from a gender perspective.

Nutrition

Using IT, women can have to know the high risk of malnutrition and disease that women face at all the three critical stages viz. infancy and childhood, adolescent and reproductive phase, focuses attention would be paid to meeting the nutritional needs of women at all stages of the life cycle. This is also important in view of the critical link between the health of adolescent girls, pregnant and lactating women to tackle the problem of macro and micro nutrient deficiencies especially amongst pregnant and lactating women as it leads to various disease and disabilities.

Preserving Tradition

Information Technology (IT) can be used in codification and dissemination of women's indigenous knowledge. Traditionally women have been the incubators and transmitters of indigenous knowledge related to growing of specific crop, preservation of seed, food processing, ethno-botanical aspects and ethno-veterinary aspects. This indigenous knowledge has scientifically sound value and effective medium like IT can help organize and transfer this knowledge to outside communities for two way benefits.

Conclusion

In the present context of rapidly changing world, where societal transformations are called for, there is no other potential tool other than information technology, for empowering the most deprived section i.e. women. An effective policy towards initiating socially acceptable, economically viable and practically feasible IT projects will be a major step in realizing the social, political and economic empowerment of women.

REFERENCES

1. http://www.isiswomen.org/onsite/ict_gender.htm.
2. Lawley, E. L. (1993): "*Computer and the Communication of Gender*". From www.undp.org/gender/resourse/.
3. Meera, S.N. and Rao, D.U.M (2003), "*IT for Empowerment of Women*", Yojana, February.
4. National Policy for the empowerment of Women (2001), Ministry of Human Resources Development, Department of Women and Child Development, www.wcd.nic.in.
5. Sharma, U. (2003), "*Women Empowerment through Information Technology,*" Authors Press, Delhi.
6. www.google.com.

Index

S

T

U

V

W

Y